Lewis Morris

Songs of Britain

Lewis Morris

Songs of Britain

ISBN/EAN: 9783337007188

Printed in Europe, USA, Canada, Australia, Japan

Cover: Foto ©Thomas Meinert / pixelio.de

More available books at **www.hansebooks.com**

BY

LEWIS MORRIS

LONDON
KEGAN PAUL, TRENCH & CO., 1, PATERNOSTER SQUARE
1887

PREFACE.

THE present volume comes so quickly after the writer's tragedy, "Gycia," published last year, that it may be well to say that the earlier poem was written as far back as the end of the year 1884.

Of the three legends from Wild Wales contained in this volume, the first is derived partly from the "Mabinogion," partly from a quasi-historical tradition. The two others follow as nearly as may be the oral traditions collected by the writer's friend, Professor Rhys, from all parts of Wales, and reproduced by him in the pages of the Cymmrodorion

Society's Journal. It should be understood that "The Physicians of Myddfai" is a poem rather than a metrical exercise, and that the writer is well aware that, without considerable indulgence in the matter of metre, English elegiac verse must be practically impossible.

Penbryn, *April*, 1887.

CONTENTS.

	PAGE
ON A THRUSH SINGING IN AUTUMN	1
IN A COUNTRY CHURCH ...	5
IN SPRING-TIDE	13
IN AUTUMN ...	15
A MIDSUMMER NIGHT'S DREAM	17
AN ENGLISH IDYLL	25
ANIMA MUNDI ...	29
IN PEMBROKESHIRE, 1886	31
EASTER-TIDE ...	37
GHOSTS ...	43
SONG	46
FROM WILD WALES:	
I. LLYN Y MORWYNION...	48
II. THE PHYSICIANS OF MYDDFAI ...	59
III. THE CURSE OF PANTANNAS	102

	PAGE
TO A GAY COMPANY ...	126
FROM JUVENAL	130
IGHTHAM MOTE ...	132
THE SECRET OF THINGS ...	138
OH, EARTH! ...	144
ON A BIRTHDAY	146
IN A GERMAN LABORATORY	149
THE SUMMONS	152
SILVERN SPEECH	154
THE OBELISK	157
A SONG OF EMPIRE ...	163

SONGS OF BRITAIN.

ON A THRUSH SINGING IN AUTUMN.

SWEET singer of the Spring, when the new world
Was filled with song and bloom, and the fresh year
Tripped, like a lamb tender and void of fear,
Through daisied grass and juicy leaves unfurled,
Where is thy liquid voice
That all day would rejoice?
Where now thy sweet and homely call,
Which from gray dawn to evening's chilling fall
Would echo from thin copse and tasselled brake,
For homely duty tuned and love's sweet sake?

The spring-tide passed, high summer soon should come.
The woods grew thick, the meads a deeper hue ;
The pipy summer growths swelled, lush and tall ;
The sharp scythes swept at daybreak through the dew.
Thou didst not heed at all,
Thy prodigal voice grew dumb ;
No more with song mightst thou beguile,
She sitting on her speckled eggs the while,
Thy mate's long vigil as the slow days went,
Solacing her with lays of measureless content.

Nay, nay, thy voice was Duty's, nor would dare
Sing were Love fled, though still the world were fair ;
The summer waxed and waned, the nights grew cold,
The sheep were thick within the wattled fold,
The woods began to moan,
Dumb wert thou and alone;
Yet now, when leaves are sere, thy ancient note

On a Thrush singing in Autumn.

Comes low and halting from thy doubtful throat.
Oh, lonely loveless voice, what dost thou here
In the deep silence of the fading year?

Thus do I read the answer of thy song:
"I sang when winds blew chilly all day long;
I sang because hope came and joy was near,
I sang a little while, I made good cheer;
In summer's cloudless day
My music died away;
But now the hope and glory of the year
Are dead and gone, a little while I sing
Songs of regret for days no longer here,
And touched with presage of the far-off Spring."

Is this the meaning of thy note, fair bird?
Or do we read into thy simple brain
Echoes of thoughts which human hearts have stirred,

High-soaring joy and melancholy pain?
Nay, nay, that lingering note
Belated from thy throat—
" Regret," is what it sings, " regret, regret!
The dear days pass, but are not wholly gone.
In praise of those I let my song go on ;
'Tis sweeter to remember than forget."

IN A COUNTRY CHURCH.

The organ peals, the people stand,
The white procession through the aisles,
As is our modern use, defiles
In ranks, which part on either hand.

They chant the psalms with resonant voice
These peasants of our Saxon Kent;
With the old Hebrew king rejoice,
With him grow contrite and repent.

But when the pale priest, blandly cold,
White-winged above the eagle bends,
I lose the ancient words of old,
The monotone which still ascends.

For there the village school is set,
A row of shining faces bright,
Round cheeks by time unwrinkled yet,
Smooth heads, and boyish collars white.

And through the row there runs a smile,
Like sunlight on a rippling sea—
A childish mirth, devoid of guile;
What may the merry movement be?

The teachers frown; not far to seek
The wonder seems, for it is this:
A little scholar whose round cheek
A stain of gules appears to kiss.

For some low shaft of wintry sun
Strikes where Dame Dorothy of the Grange,
In long devotions never done,
Kneels on through centuries of change;

And from her robe's unfading rose,
Athwart the fair heads ranged below,
A ruddy shaft at random goes,
And lights them with unwonted glow.

And straightway all the scene but these
Grows dim for me; I heed no more
The preacher's smooth monotonies,
The chants repeated o'er and o'er.

For I am borne on fancy's wings
Far from the Present to the Past;
From those which pass to those which last,
The root and mystery of Things.

How many an old and vanished day
Has gone, she kneeling there the while,
And watching, with her saintly smile,
The generations fade away.

The children came each Sunday there
To hear the self-same chant and hymn ;
The boys grew strong, the girls grew fair,
Their lives with fleeting years grew dim.

Their children's children came and went,
She kneeling in the self-same prayer ;
They passed to withered age, and bent,
And left the Lady kneeling there.

They passed, and on the churchyard ground
No more their humble names are seen ;
Only upon the billowy mound
Yearly the untrodden grass grows green.

They grew, they waned through toil and strife,
From innocence to guilt and sin ;
They gained what prize was theirs to win,
They sank in shame the load of life.

And still the kneeling Lady calm
Throws gules on many a childish head,
And still the self-same prayers are said,
The self-same chant, the self-same psalm.

So had they been, before as yet,
Her far-off grandsires lived and died,
Ere long descent had nourished pride,
Before the first Plantagenet.

No change, unless some change there were
In simpler rite or grayer stone,
The self-same worship never done,
And for its very age grown fair.

Great God, the creatures of Thy hand,
Must they thus fail for ever still
Thy high behests to understand,
To seek and find Thy hidden will?

Are Thy hands slow to succour then?
And are Thy eyes, then, slow to see
The toiling, tempted race of men
Born into sin and misery?

For nineteen centuries of Time,
Nay more, for dim unnumbered years,
Men's gaze have sought Thy face sublime,
And turned uncomforted, in tears.

For countless years unsullied youth
Has sunk through grosser mire of sense;
And yet men cherish innocence!
And yet we are no nearer truth!

And not the less from age to age
Heavenward the unchanging suffrage rolls
From hearts inspired by holy rage,
And meek and uncomplaining souls,

In a Country Church.

Who see no cloud of doubt o'erspread
The far horizons of the sky,
But view with clear, undoubting eye
The mansions of the happy dead.

Oh, wonder ! oh, perplexèd thought !
Oh, interchange of good and ill !
In vain, by life's long pain untaught,
We strive to solve the riddle still.

In vain, so mixed the twofold skein,
That none the tangle may unwind ;
Where one the gate of Heaven may find,
Another shrinks in hopeless pain.

So here the immemorial sum
Of simple reverence may breed
A finer worship than might come
For fruit of some severer creed.

Kneel, Lady, blazoned in thy place!
Through generations children kneel.
To know is weaker than to feel:
Though Truth seem far, we know her face!

IN SPRING-TIDE.

    This is the hour, the day,
    The time, the season sweet.
    Quick! hasten, laggard feet,
    Brook not delay;
Love flies, youth passes, Maytide will not last;
Forth, forth, while yet 'tis time, before the Spring is past.

    The Summer's glories shine
    From all her garden ground,
    With lilies prankt around,
    And roses fine;
But the pink blooms or white upon the bursting trees,
Primrose and violet sweet, what charm has June like
    these?

This is the time of song.
From many a joyous throat,
Mute all the dull year long,
Soars love's clear note;
Summer is dumb, and faint with dust and heat;
This is the mirthful time when every sound is sweet.

Fair day of larger light,
Life's own appointed hour,
Young souls bud forth in white—
The world's a-flower;
Thrill, youthful heart; soar upward, limpid voice;
Blossoming time is come—rejoice, rejoice, rejoice!

IN AUTUMN.

"Decay, decay," the wildering west winds cry,
"Decay, decay," the moaning woods reply;
The whole dead autumn landscape, drear and chill,
Strikes the same chord of desolate sadness still.
The drifting clouds, the floods a sullen sea,
The dead leaves whirling from the ruined tree,
The rain which falling soaks the sodden way,
Proclaim the parting summer's swift decay.
No song of bird, nor joyous sight or thing,
Which smooths the wintry forefront of the spring;
No violet lurking in its mossy bed,
Nor drifted snow-bloom bending overhead,

Nor kingcups carpeting the meads with gold,
Nor tall spiked orchids purpling all the wold;
But thin dull herbage which no more may grow,
And dry reeds rustling as the chill winds blow,
Bleak hillsides whence the huddled flocks are fled,
And every spear of crested grass lies dead.
" Decay, decay," the leafless woodlands sigh,
The torpid earth, and all the blinded sky,
And down the blurred moor, 'mid the dying day,
An age-worn figure limps its weary way.

A MIDSUMMER NIGHT'S DREAM.

FAR in the west sinks down the Sun
On bars of violet and gold,
A soft breeze springs up fresh and cold,
And darkness a transparent pall
Upon the waiting earth begins to fall,
And, decked with countless gems of lucent light,
Walks forth the sable Night,
And once again the unfailing miracle is done.

Ineffable, illimitable, immense,
Wonder of wonders, mystery of Space,
How can a finite vision meet thy face?

How shall not our poor eyes, dazzled and dim,
Which see but thy vast circle's outward rim,
Sink touched before thy gaze with impotence?
How shall our feeble voices dare to hymn
Thy infinite glories—voices which were best
To mortal loves and earth's poor joys addrest?
How seek our earthly limits to transcend,
And, without halt or pause,
Soaring beyond the limit of our laws,
Touch with a feeble hand on glories without end?

  Nay, great are these indeed
And infinite, but not so great as He
Their Maker who has formed them, who made me,
Who can in fancy leap, outward and outward still
Beyond our System and its farthest star,
Beyond the greater Systems ranged afar,
To which our faintest suns are satellites, and no more—

Beyond, beyond, beyond, till mind can fill
The illimitable void which never sense
Nor thought alone may compass or contain,
And with a whirling brain
Return to the great Centre of all light,
Which doth control and bound the Infinite,
And, looking to the undiscovered Sun,
Find all perplexity and longing done,
And am content to wonder and to adore.

   This 'tis alone
Which doth console and soothe our feeble thought,
Faint with the too great strain to comprehend
An Infinite Creation without end.
Wherever through the boundless wastes we stray,
For ever and for ever, some faint ray
Of the great central Sun, the hidden Will,
Attends our wanderings still;

Beyond the utmost limits of the sky,
Unseen, yet seen, the gaze of an Eternal Eye.
No waste of systems lies around,
But a great Rule by which all things are bound.
A changeless order circles sun with sun;
One great Will pulses through, and makes them one.
System on system, vast or small,
One great Intelligence directs them all.
No longer from the endless maze we shrink,
Like those who on some sea-cliff's dreadful brink
Long to fling down into the empty air
And lose the pain of living, and to be
Sunk in the deep abysses of the sea;
To lose the pain of living and the care,
Which dogs life like its shadow.
      Nay, no dread
Have we who know a great Sun overhead,
Which shines upon us always, unbeheld.

How should our eyes behold what is too great
For our imperfect state?
How should our minds reach to it; how attain
With a too feeble brain,
To comprehend the Unbounded, the Immense,
Incomprehensible by finite sense?—
How through the Finite view the Infinite,
Except by this clear Light?

   That is the light, indeed,
Which lights all souls which come upon the earth.
That is the central Sun which on our birth
Shone, and will shine upon us till the end;
A central Will which holds the worlds in space;
A Presence, though we look not on its face,
Which sows a cosmic order through the waste of things;
A Being, all the beatings of whose wings
Are secular wastes of Time; of whose great soul

Creations are but moods, in whose vast mind
Antinomies of Thought repose combined,
Till those which seem to us as changeless laws
Show but as phases of the Unchanging Cause,
And we and all things fade and pass away,
Lost in the effulgence of the Boundless Day.

    Let, then, unbounded Space,
Sown thick with worlds, encompass us; we care
No whit for it, nor shall our dazzled eyes
This waste of Worlds surprise,
Which have looked on its Maker, who is more
Than all his work can be, but not the less
Dwells in each human soul that looks on Him
Albeit with vision dim;
Whose constant Presence all our lives confess,
Of whom we are a part, and closer far
Than is the farthest, most unmeasured star,

Than are His great suns, big with fruitful strife,
Seeing that we are a portion of His Life,
Seeing that we hold His Essence—some clear spark,
Which shines when all creation else grows dark,
And are, however impotent and small,
One with the Will that made and governs all.

  * * * * *

 And now the night grows thin;
A subtle air of dawning seems to stir
Before the dawn, as if its harbinger
To prisoned souls within,
Proclaiming the near coming of the day.
Then Darkness, a great bird, with raven wing,
Flies to the furthest west, and in her stead
Young Day, an orient conqueror overhead,
Looks down, and all that waste of worlds has fled;
And once again the Eternal, mystic Birth
Is born upon the earth,

And once again the round of wholesome life,
The doubt-dispelling stir and joyous strife,
Chases the dreadful visions of the night,
Lost in the increasing light;
And from the spheres a still voice seems to say,
"Awake, arise, adore, behold the Day!
It is enough to be, nor question why;
It is enough to work our work and die;
It is enough to feel and not to know.
Behold, the Dawn is breaking; let us go."

AN ENGLISH IDYLL.

ONCE I remember, in a far-off June,
Leaving the studious cloister of my youth,
Beside the young Thames' stream I laid me down,
Wearied, upon a bank. 'Twas midsummer;
The warm earth teemed with flowers; the kingcup's gold,
The perfumed clover, 'mid the crested grass,
The plantains rearing high their flowery crowns
Above the daisied coverts; overhead,
The hawthorns, white and rosy, bent with bloom,
The broad-spread chestnuts spiked with frequent flowers,
And white gold-hearted lilies on the stream;

All these made joy within my heart, and woke
The fair idyllic phantasies of Greece ;
And dreaming, well content with the rich charm
Of summer England, long I idly mused :
" And were the deep-set vales of Thessaly
Or fair Olympian beech-groves more than this ?
Or the Sicilian meads more rich in flowers,
Where the lost goddess plucked the asphodel ?
Or flowed the clear stream through a lovelier shade
Where Dian bathed and rapt Actæon saw ?
Or were they purer depths where Hylas played
Till the nymphs drew him down ? Ah, fairer dreams
Than our poor England holds ! Grave, toil-worn land !
Poor agèd mother of a graceless brood,
With shambling gait and limbs by labour bent !
What should she know of such ? "

        When straight I heard
A ripple of boyish mirth, and looking saw

Far off along the meads a gliding boat
Float noiselessly; lithe forms at either end—
The self-same forms which Phidias fixed of old—
With tall poles, pressed it forward, others lay
Reclined, and all had crowned their short smooth hair
With lilies from the stream, while one had shaped
Some hollow reed in semblance of a pipe,
Making a shrill faint sound—a joyous crew,
Clothed with the grace of innocent nakedness.
Then, while they yet were far, ere yet a sound
Of their poor rustic tones assailed the sense,
Or too great nearness marred the grace of form——

Poised sudden in a white row, side by side,
They plunged down headlong in the sweet warm tide.
Then, as I went, within myself I said,
" The young Apollo is not wholly fled,

Nor can long centuries of toil and care
Make youth less comely or the earth less fair.
To the world's ending Joy and Grace shall be.
I, too, have been to-day in Arcady."

ANIMA MUNDI.

Oh great World-Spirit, wherefore art thou come?
We crave an answer, but thy voice is dumb.

Oh great World-Spirit, whither dost thou tend?
By what dark paths to what mysterious end?

We do not know, we cannot tell at all,
Only before thy onward march we fall.

  * * * * *

Nay, but before thy throne we fall, we kneel;
We crave not that thy face thou shouldst reveal;
We do not seek to know, only to feel.

We praise thee not in words our tongues can tell;
Though thy hand slay us, we will not rebel.
Whate'er thy will design for us, 'tis well.

Compute our lives with all thy boundless past,
Project them on thy abysmal Future vast;
Only let all be merged in Thee at last.

IN PEMBROKESHIRE, 1886.

THROUGH crested grass I took my way
From my loved home. The sun was high ;
The warm air slept the live-long day ;
No shadowy cloudlet veiled the sky.

The swift train swept with rhythmic tune,
By endless pastures hurrying down,
White farm, lone chapel, castled town,
Then, fringed with weed, the salt lagune.

And last the land-locked haven blue.
Thin-sown with monstrous works of war,
And on the sweet salt air I knew
Faint sounds of cheering from afar.

*   *   *   *   *

Strong arms and backs are bent, and then
They draw us up the fluttering street;
Behind, there comes the ordered beat
Of long-drawn files of marching men.

At last a halt; a steep hillside
Set thick with toil-worn workers strong,
Grave faces stretching far and wide,
Fired with the hope to banish wrong.

Ah me! how thin one voice appears,
To reach so many eager minds!
Nay, for it speaks to willing ears,
And what the hearer seeks he finds.

Unhappy Island of the West!
Thy brethren these in race and blood,
Not like thee tempted or opprest,
But filled with longing for thy good.

In Pembrokeshire, 1886.

For just is manhood rude and strong
And generous the toiler's soul;
When these the ship of State control,
Oppression shall not flourish long.

*   *   *   *   *

The crowds are gone, the hillside bare,
The last good-nights at length are said,
The harbour crossed again, the fair
Large star of eve hangs overhead.

The shades of tardy evening fall;
Lights come in casements here and there;
Through dewy meads on the cool air
The wandering landrails hoarsely call.

The silent roads loom ghostly white;
No veil of darkness hides the skies;
A sunless dawn appears to rise
Upon the stilly charmèd night.

The day's hot concourse comes to seem
Far, far away; the eager crowd,
The upturned gaze, the plaudits loud,
In the cool silence like a dream.

And oh, sweet odours, which the air
Of the calm summer midnight deep
Draws from the rose which lies asleep,
And bowery honeysuckles fair.

Oh, perfumed night! Some tremulous bird
From the thick hedgerows seems to thrill.
No other sound but this is heard,
Save ringing horsehoofs, beating still.

Midnight is past; there comes a gleam,
Precursor of the scarce-set sun.
Through gray streets hushed as in a dream
We sweep, and the long day is done.

* * * * *

In Pembrokeshire, 1886.

Men pass, but still shall Nature keep
Her night's cool calm, her dawn's bright glow;
Unseen her fragrant wild flowers creep,
Unmarked her midnight odours blow.

The long injustices of years
Shall pass; the hapless Western Isle
Shall dry the age-long trace of tears,
And show instead a happy smile.

The wheels of Fate are swiftly borne
From point to point, from change to change;
What yesterday was new and strange
To-morrow scouts as old and worn.

I may forget the shouting crowd,
The sea of eyes which upward turn,
The kindling cheeks, the plaudits loud,
The sympathies which glow and burn.

Ay, all things change, but hardly those
Shall fade—the midnight calm of June,
The cool sweet airs, the night-bird's tune,
The perfume of the sleeping rose.

EASTER-TIDE.

    Awake, arise, oh Earth!
    Thy hour has come at last;
    The winter's ruin past,
    Spring comes to birth.
The virgin world with flowers again grows bright,
And in the increasing light
Doth clothe herself with beauty; once again
A new creation issues with a stately train.

    Oh soul of man, arise
    And keep thy Easter-tide,
    White clothed as is a bride,
    With calm pure eyes;

When all things living else rejoice,
Not thine should be the voice
Alone to keep dull silence, mute, unheard,
Amid the joy that wakens every nesting bird.

'Tis an old Spring of mirth
That bids our souls arise;
No other moved the priests and augurs wise
Upon the younger earth
When for the Passover the lamb was slain,
Nor when they did complain
Of old time for the fair Adonis dead,
Greeting with tears of joy that dear recovered head.

The same, yet not the same,
Joy fuller, deeper grief
Than in the old ages came
To wake belief.

Easter-tide.

The Spring our voices celebrate to-day
Is not the Spring which fades with May,
Nor that renewal ours which shall be done
Soon as our earth leans outward from the averted sun.

    Nor as theirs is our loss
    Who wept the enamoured boy;
    Ours is a heavier cross,
    A livelier joy,
Mixed in such sort with grief that one is bred
From the others and by it nourishèd,
So that without the salutary pain
Were no place left for this triumphant gain.

    Great Law of Sacrifice
    On which our lives are built,
    That with our load of guilt
    Soars to the skies,

I doubt if ever there was race of man
But based its life on such a mystic plan,
From old Prometheus' godlike treachery
To calm Osiris cold and sad Persephone.

    Therefore, because the end
    Of Winter comes and Death,
    Our yearning souls ascend,
    Faith quickeneth.

How should it be that man alone could cease
When all things else increase?
Man, the first fruit of Time, Creation's crown—
Shall he, while all is Spring, lie hopeless and cast down?

    Ay, always with the Spring
    The waking comes again;
    Mixed tones of joy and pain
    Our life-chords sing.

Easter-tide.

Sweet are the songs of autumn, sweet of death,
And bitter sweet the first-drawn breath,
And sweet, though full of pain, the mortal strife
When from Death's grasp we struggle into Life

  That is the law of life—
  Joy bought by sacrifice,'
  Pleasure for hopeless sighs,
  And rest for strife.
The earth is no more, as it was at first,
By some strange spell accurst ;
A mystery has passed a mystery,
A boundless hope has bid new heavens and earth
 to be.

  Rise, happy Earth, arise,
  Thy wintry darkness done,
  To greet the new-risen sun
  Oh soul, arise !

The joy which stirs the world let it wake thee.
A symbol of thy risen life is born.
Awake, arise! this is the very morn;
A mystery has been! a mystery!

GHOSTS.

Sometimes in some forsaken place,
    Hid from the aspect of the sun,
We come on some forgotten trace
    Of life and years long dead and done.

Some faded picture's doubtful truth,
    Fixed in the springtime of our days,
Which through all change of mien portrays
    The evanescent charm of youth—

The rounded cheek, the wealth of hair,
    The bright young eye's unclouded blue.
White head, wan face, were you thus fair?
    Sad eyes, and were these ever you?

Changed, and yet still unchanged through change,
    The self-same lives for good or ill,
Thin ghosts with features known, yet strange,
    Of us who live and travail still.

Thin ghosts! or is it we who fade
    And are deceased, and keep no more
Than some thin unsubstantial shade
    Of the young hopes and fears of yore?

Who knows what Life, or Death, or Time
    Are in themselves, or whither tend
The great world's footsteps slow, sublime,
    From what dim source—to what hidden end?

Or if our growth be but decay,
    Or if all Life must wax and grow,
Or if no change true Being know,
    Though all things outward pass away?

Ghosts.

Ah! not in outward things we know
    The chiefest work of Time and Change;
But new faiths come, old thoughts grown strange,
    Old longings which no more may glow.

Some time-stained sheaf of youthful verse,
    Some inarticulate yearning dumb,
Once dear, ere time and age had come
    To turn the better to the worse.

In these the gazer starts to see
    A self, not his, reflected most,
And asking, "Were these part of me?"
    Knows he has looked upon a ghost.

SONG.

Love took my life and thrilled it
   Through all its strings,
Played round my mind and filled it
   With sound of wings,
But to my heart he never came
To touch it with his golden flame.

Therefore it is that singing
   I do rejoice,
Nor heed the slow years bringing
   A harsher voice,
Because the songs which he has sung
Still leave the untouched singer young.

Song.

But whom in fuller fashion
   The Master sways,
For him, swift winged with passion,
   Fleet the brief days.
Betimes the enforcèd accents come,
And leave him ever after dumb.

FROM WILD WALES.

I.

LLYN Y MORWYNION.

By fair Festiniog, 'mid the Northern Hills,
The vales are full of beauty, and the heights,
Thin-set with mountain sheep, show statelier far
Than in the tamer South.   There the stern round
Of labour rules,—a silent land, sometimes
Loud with the blast that buffets all the hills
Whereon the workers toil, in quarries hewn
Upon the terraced rocksides.   Tier on tier,
Above the giddy depths, they edge and cling
Like flies to the sheer precipice as they strike
The thin cleft slate.   For solace of their toil

Song comes to strengthen them, and songlike verse
In the old Cymric measures, and the dream
Of fame when all the listening thousands round
Are ranged in Session, and the rapt array
Expectant of the singer's soaring voice,
Or full quire rising thund'rous to the skies,
The sheathed swords, and the sacred Chair of oak,
Where sits the Bard. But most of all they prize
Old memories of the Past, forgotten feuds,
And battles long ago. One tale they tell
Of a deep tarn upon the mountain side,
Llyn y Morwynion called,—" The Maidens' Lake ;"
And thus it is the fair old story runs.

On Arvon once the men of Meirion,
Being alone, nor having hearth or home,
Swooped down when all her warriors were afield

Against the foemen. And they snatched from them
The flower of all the maidens of the race,
And to their mountain fastness far away
Bare them unchecked. There with great care and love
They tended them, and in the captives' hearts
The new observance slowly ousted all
The love of home and country, till they stayed
Content, forgetting all their lives before,
Parents and kinsfolk, everything but love.

 But when the war was ended, and their arms
Set free, the men of Arvon sent demand
That they should straight restore to home and kin
The maidens they had rapt. Then came great doubt
Upon the men of Meirion, knowing well
Their strength too weak to match the Arvonian hosts
In unassisted war; heralds they sent
To Arvon asking peace, making amends

For what had been their fault. But the others nursed
Deep anger in their hearts, and to their words
Made only answer, " Give ye back untouched
Our daughters and our sisters, whom your fraud
Has stolen from us, or prepare to die."
Then they, taking deep counsel with themselves,
Swore not for life itself would they return
The women, only if themselves should will
To leave them ; and they made request of them
That they might know their wish. But when they sought
To question them, they answered with one voice—

"We will not go ; for barren is the lot
Of maidenhood, and cold the weary fate
Of loveless lives, the household tasks whose weight
Bears down the childless woman. Since we came
We have known life in the full light of home.
Say to our sires and brothers, that we stay

Willing, and bid our young men that they wive
From out some noble tribe; for thus it is
Our Cymric race grows strong. But do ye bid
Our mothers comfort them, for they shall take
Their grandsons on their knees; for we are wed
And cannot more return. Not Fate itself
Can e'er recall the irrevocable Past."

But when the men of Arvon heard the hest
The herald brought, their souls were wroth in them
Against the ravishers, whose cunning wiles
Had worked such wrong. They called their warriors forth
From every hill and dale, and marched in haste
To Meirion. And they summoned them to yield,
But they would not; and so the fight was set
For the morrow, on the margin of a mere
Deep down within the circuit of the hills.

Llyn y Morwynion.

There, with the sun, within a close-set pass
The men of Meirion stood, a scanty band,
Waiting the approaching host. With grief and pain
They left their loves, and swift, with breaking day,
Marched with unfaltering steps, without a word,
To the field of honour, as men go who know
That all beside is lost. But as they stood,
Ranged in stern silence, waiting for the fray,
They saw a white procession thread the pass
Behind, now seen, now lost, by flowery bends,
Gorse gold and heather purple. At their head
Blodeuwedd, she the flower in face and form
By magic formed, by magical art foredoomed
To sin and suffer. Then again they knew
The bitterness of death, and clasped once more
The forms they loved, when by the lake the sun
Lit the fierce light of countless marching spears.

Then with a last embrace the tearful throng
Withdrew to where above the fastness rose
A purple slope. No way the assailing host
Might find to it while yet one stalwart arm
Of Meirion lived. Toward the lake it fell,
Till in a sheer, precipitous cliff it sank,
Its base in the unfathomable deep.

Now, while the maidens like a fleece of cloud
Whitened the hill, or like a timid flock
From nearer danger shrinking, swift there came
Along the grassy margin of the lake
The countless spears of Arvon. And their sires
And brethren saw them, and great wrath and joy
Fired them and urged them onward, till they surged
And broke on Meirion. But her strong sons stood
And flung them backward; and the frightened throng
Of white-robed suppliants saw the deed, and feared,

Hiding their eyes, hovering 'twixt hope and fear,
Divided 'twixt their lovers and their kin.

   All day the battle raged, from morn to eve;
All day the men of Arvon charged and broke,
And charged again the little band which stood
Unshaken in the pass, but hourly grew
Weaker and weaker still. But at the last
The noise of battle ceased awhile; the shouts,
The cries, grew silent. On the purple hill
The kneeling women saw the Arvonian host
Retreating with their dead, and rose to go
With succour to their lovers. As they gazed,
Sudden, as with a last despairing strength
And a hoarse shout, again, a torrent of steel,
The men of Arvon, by their own weight pressed,
Burst on the scant defenders of the pass;
Like some fierce surge which from the storm-vext sea,

Through narrow inlets fenced by rocky walls,
Lifts high its furious crest, and sweeps in ruin
Within the rayless, haunted ocean caves,
Rocks, wreckage, and the corpses of the dead.

  And as the women, impotent to save,
With agonizing hands and streaming eyes
Looked down upon the pass, they saw their loves
Driven back, o'erwhelmed, surrounded, flashing swords
And thrusting spears and broken shields, and heard
The noise of desperate battle, then a pause
And silence, as the last of Meirion's sons
Sank in his blood and the long fight was done.

  Then suddenly, ere yet the conquering host
Might climb to them, Blodeuwedd, standing clothed
In her unearthly beauty, faced the throng
Of shrinking women. Not a word she spake.

The sinking sun upon her snowy robe
Shone with unearthly gold; like some fair bird
Leading the flock she showed. With one white arm
She pointed to the dreadful pass where lay
The thick-piled corpses, with the other signed
Toward the sheer cliff, and to the lake beneath
Motioned. One word she uttered—" Follow me,"
And all who heard it knew and shared her mind.

Then looking to the heavens, she hurried down
Through thyme and heather, chanting some wild hymn
To the Immortal Gods; and with her went
The white-robed throng, and when they gained the
    verge,
Without a pause, plunged through the empty air
Into the unfathomed depths, like some great flight
Of white birds swooping from a sea-cliff down
To ocean. The still waters leapt in foam;

One loud shriek only woke the air, and then
Silence was over all, and night and death.

Still sometimes, when the dreaming peasants go
By the lone mountain tarn at shut of day,
The white clouds with the eve descending swift
Down the steep hillside to the lake may seem
The white-robed maidens falling, and the shriek
Of night birds, fair Blodeuwedd and her train ;
And fancy, by the ancient fable fed,
Turns from the duller Present's dust and glare
To the enchanted twilights of the Past.

II.

THE PHYSICIANS OF MYDDFAI.

Far, far away in wild Wales, by the shore of the boundless Atlantic,
Where the cloud-capt peaks of the North are dwarfed to the hills of the South,
And through the long vale to the sea, the full-fed, devious Towy
Turns and returns on itself, like the coils of a silvery snake,
A grey town sits up aloft on the bank of the clear, flowing river,
As it has sat since the days when the Roman was first in the land.

A town, with a high ruined castle and walls mantled over with ivy,
With church towers square and strong and narrow irregular streets,
And, frequent in street and lane, many-windowed high-shouldered chapels,
Whence all the still Sabbath ascend loud preaching and passionate prayer,
Such violent wrestling with sin, that the dogs on the pavement deserted
Wake with a growl from their dreams at the sound of the querulous voice,
And the gay youths, released from the counter and bound for the seaside or hillside,
Start as they wake on their way echoes of undevout feet's,
And here and there a rude square, with statues of popular heroes,

A long quay with scarcely a ship, and a hoary bridge
  spanning the stream,
The stream which struggles in June by the shallows
  where children are swimming,
The furious flood which at Yule roars seaward, resistless
  along,
Though the white steam ribbons float by it, forlorn it
  seems, almost forsaken.
All the day long in the week the dumb streets are
  hushed in repose,
But on market or fair days there comes a throng of
  Welsh-speaking peasants
From many a lonely farm in the folds of the rain-beaten
  hills,
And the long streets are filled with the high-pitched
  speech of the chaffering Cymry,
With a steeple-crowned hat, here and there, and the red
  cloaks which daunted the French.

Scarce in Keltic Britanny's self, or in homely Teutonic Silesia,
So foreign a crowd may you see as in this far corner of Wales.

Above the grey old town, at the mouth of the exquisite valley,
Rises a quaint village church deep in o'ershadowing yews;
On a round-topped hill it stands, looking down on the silvery river
And the smooth meadows fenced by tall elms, and the black kine, like flies on the green.
Below, midst its smooth-pleached lawns, stands the many-roofed Anglican palace,
And aloft from its straight-ridged pines, the enchanter's summit ascends.
Thence along the upward vale, by fold upon fold of the river

By park and by tower, at last the far-off mountain chains soar,
Flecked with shadow and sunshine which float on the side of the desolate moorland,
And the whole still landscape lies bathed in a haze of ineffable peace.

There, where the mountains ascend by the white little town of Llandovery,
Steeply the circular side of the crater-like summit dips down.
A blue lake lies beneath, deep set in the desolate hollow,
Where scarcely a breath of air ruffles in summer its face.
The Van Lake 'tis called of old time, like the Van Lake of distant Armenia.
Hardly a wayfarer's foot comes near, or a wayfarer's eye.

But far, far below are seen the white homesteads, dotting the valley,
And to-day, as of old, still silence and solitude everywhere reign.

There, as in crowded towns, life is real and full of striving;
There, too, is life fulfilled of small hopes and of trivial fears.
There, too, the finger of fate, unavoidable, pitiless, awful,
Points with unfaltering aim, to the road which our footsteps shall tread.
Love is among them, and hate, low desires and high aspirations,
Fortune is blind there as here, the good mourn, and the wicked rejoice.
Only there the sense of the Past, the romantic, the mystical lingers,

Touched with a glamour and charm, denied to the turmoil of towns.
The light which never has been, still shines on those hillsides secluded
Illuming with rays, not of earth, those homely and labouring lives.
Here is a tale which is cherished to-day through that far-withdrawn valley,
Half believed by the agèd folk still, but year by year fading away.

Long, long ago, when our Princes were falling in fight with the Norman,
And all our wild Wales lay o'erwhelmed by a torrent of rapine and blood,

A brave peasant woman strove here with hard fate, though her husband had fallen,
Strove for her only boy, who was rising to manhood apace.
So close was the bond which bound widowed mother and dutiful stripling,
None of Myddfai's daughters touched the young man's self-contained heart.
A kindly fortune smiled on the toil of the desolate woman,
Their flocks and their herds increased on the meads of the bountiful vale,
So quickly their numbers grew, that from the shorn valley he drove them
To fresh fields and pastures new on the side of the mystical hills.

    Morning and evening he watched on the lonely side of the hollow,
While the grey kine wandered at will on the hill's half-precipitous steep.

Oft on the lake's still surface, no breath came to ruffle the mirror,
Nor sound, save the boulders rolled downward, that stirred for a moment its calm.
All the day long he mused, wrapt in thought on the desolate hillside,
All day the sure-footed kine cropt the sweet grass of the hills.
Thoughts came to him, innocent thoughts of a chaste youth guileless of error,
Thoughts of a maiden as fair as a young man's passionate dream.

Fair were the maidens of Myddfai, but fairer his far-off ideal,
Which touched with a glamour of gold the day-dreams of innocent youth.
All the day long he dreamt on, gazing down on the blue of the waters,

Till the plash of the trout, as they rose, seemed the oar
    of some mystical bark ;
All the day long he mused, and with evening, by moon-
    light or starlight,
Dreaming he wound his slow way with his kine to the
    valley below,
Dreaming through fair summer days and the long dark
    evenings of winter
The sweet shy dreams of a youth fulfilled of a virginal
    shame.
In secret his mother noted the dreams which her son
    was dreaming,
Marking the far-off look in the absent eyes of the boy.
Fain would she rouse him with jests and bantering words,
    but the stripling
Smiled a soft smile in reply, then turned to his musings
    again.

When he had spent many days in happy and undisturbed dreaming,
One day, as the setting sun threw beams of bright gold on the lake,
Lo ! a great marvel and wonder, a herd of phantom-like oxen
Seemed to his dazzled eyes to emerge from the mystical depths,
White they were, brindled and white, heavy dewlapped, lords of the meadows,
Driven as it seemed by a swan from the lake's far centre along,
Nearer and nearer they drew, till the swan to his yearning vision
Grew to a maiden as fair as the fanciful Fair of his dreams.
Gold were her locks and blue her eyes as the clear sky of autumn,

White was her bosom and red the half-opened rose of her mouth.
Nearer and nearer she came, till the youth, with ineffable longing,
Stretched forth his passionate arms to fold to his bosom the Fair,
   Stretched forth, and offered her bread in humble token of friendship;
But the Fair smiled a sweet smile, smiled and eluded his grasp.
Then, as he stood on the brink, in mute and motionless yearning,
Lo! with a silvery laugh, the fair vision faded away.

   Oftentimes thus on the brink he stood afterwards waiting the maiden,
Often she came not at all, or a strong wind ruffled the deep.

Twice again did she come, and he held forth bread for
    her taking,
Still, with a silvery laugh, refusing, she faded away.

    Careworn the young man grew, and spent with un-
    satisfied yearnings,
Nor recked though the kine unheeded strayed on the
    perilous steeps.
Never again the lake maiden came by sunlight or moon-
    light,
Till his fond hope too long deferred, wasted him body and
    soul.
All his sleepless nights were filled with the pitiless vision;
All the musing days, a slow fire burned in his breast;
Half ashamed, he told his mother his pain, and the
    pitying woman
Sighed that her son should thus pine, but knew not to
    succour his grief,

Marking his cheeks' red flush, she feared lest her son might be taken,
Till she found no heart for her toil, and her substance wasted away.

There, when Midsummer Eve was come, the magical season,
The young man wandered in vain on the brink of the mystical lake;
There, when All-Hallow-tide came, he wandered, if only the maiden
Might rise on his longing eyes; but never at all did she come.
At last, on the year's last night, he, stealthily rising at midnight,
To the cold lake side went, hopeless, with faltering feet.
The full moon bathed in silver steep hillside and slumbering waters.

By the cold lake side he paused, with something of half-renewed hope,
When, borne on the face of the waters, behold by the reeds of the lake side
Floating a magical disc of milk-white mystical bread.
Swift, yet with reverence too, as one taking the Host at the altar,
Kneeling, the youth partook of the strange ineffable food,
Till ere the strange rite was ended, again a marvellous portent
Greeted his longing eyes, and stayed the quick throb of his heart,
For on the silvery path of the moon on the undisturbed waters,
The herd that he saw once before came slowly gliding to land,
And beyond them—oh, vision of bliss!—the maid of his dreams, approaching,

Plying a light golden oar, in a swift-moving shallop of gold.
Nearer she came and more near, while his heart stood still with emotion,
Fearing the glorious dream once again should vanish away;
Nearer and nearer she came, and leaped from the skiff to the lake side,
And lay, in unearthly beauty, willingly clasped in his arms.

When he found tongue to speak, "Oh, my love, at last have I found thee!
Though not of earth is thy race, oh, stoop to my virginal love.
Oh, it is long I have loved thee, and though I know thee immortal,
Tarry awhile, fair vision, leave me not loveless again!
Come from thy mountain heights, come from thy dwelling deep down in the waters.

Pity me ere I die who can only live in thy love."

Then the maid, " Rhiwallon, I love thee ; long time have I tried thy devotion,

Long have I pitied thy vigils spent in these desolate hills ;

Always have I been near thee, unseen have I witnessed thy yearnings,

Only the mystical bread was wanting to join us in one.

Now we are one heart and soul, I will live with thee always, and love thee."

And together the mystical bread they ate, and their lives were made one.

Then said the maiden, " Oh, mortal ! this warning I needs must give thee.

Thy wife will I be all thy days—thy dear wife, faithful and true,

Nourish thy children, obey thee in all things, be dutiful always,

Fill all thy fields with the dowry thou seest of full-uddered kine,
Love thee and cherish thee always, and plenish thy barn with good harvests,
Long as the will of high Heaven gives thee to live upon earth.
Only, this ordinance holds if a maid of the race of immortals
Wed with a mortal on earth, leaving her higher estate,
If he should strike her three times, she and hers, her bonds be'ng loosened,
Whether she will it or not, return to her kindred again."
Careless the fond youth heard, and smothered her warning with kisses,
And down through the joyous New Year he went with his bride to their home.

Long in great welfare they lived, knit together in happy wedlock;
Never a cloud arose on the tranquil sky of their home,
The great herds throve and increased more than all the herds of the valley,
The robbers who harried the vale left them untouched and in peace.
Never was husband more fond of the wife of his boyish affection,
Never was wife more sweet, or fuller of dutiful love.
The good mother died full of years, and calling her daughter blessèd.
Children were born of their love, more than others prudent and fair.
Their strong sons were good and discreet, laborious, eager for knowledge,
Scarcely the Abbot himself equalled their learning, 'twas said;

Fair were the daughters and good, sweet, dutiful maidens,
and prudent;
Nowhere in all our wild Wales was a race so gracious and
fair.

And yet, when their wedlock was new, that had hap-
pened which now was forgotten.
The young man and his wife were bidden one day to a
christening feast.
The young husband hastened to go; but the wife, with
half-hid reluctance,
Loitered till almost too late to traverse the difficult hills.
Many a pretext she urged, not loving the rites of
religion,
Holding some primitive faith, old as the hills and the
seas,
Till, when the hour was grown late, Rhiwallon in play-
ful impatience,

Seeking his wife up and down, found her reluctant at last.
"Come," said he, "wife, it is time," and smilingly on her fair shoulder
Tapped with his empty glove, and she rose and obeyed with a sigh.
"Dearest, remember," she said, "my warning when first we were wedded ;
Once that has been which should not. Remember, be careful, my heart !"
Then to the christening she went, nor shrank from the priest nor the water,
Only a vague disquietude long time troubled their souls.

Also long years after this, when the past was wellnigh forgotten,
They were bidden together again to a gay marriage feast in the vale ;

Not now was the wife unwilling, but ready to go and
 eager.
In deep contentment the pair went forth to the innocent
 feast.
Duly the marriage sped, the priest said his mystical
 office,
No word the good wife spake, as she knelt in her place
 by her lord;
But when the marriage was done, and they sate at the
 jovial bride-feast,
Sudden the good man perceived his wife in a passion of
 tears;
Sobbing, she sate by his side inconsolable, loudly lamenting,
Till all the gay company rose with dismay from the midst
 of their mirth.
Always her prescient soul saw the future hidden from
 mortals,

The grief that should come of that day, the dreadful problems of life,
The lives that from that day's mirth should arise—to what fate predestined?
The long generations of men foredoomed to sorrow alone.
Knowing the fever of life and its ending, the mystical woman
Held not her peace, but burst forth in a passion of weeping and pain;
But Rhiwallon, knowing not all, but filled with distress for the bridefolk,
Turned to her, and bidding her cease, touched lightly her arm in reproof.
In one moment she ceased from her wailing, and scarcely regarding her goodman,
"Love," she said, "that was the second time; only one other remains."

All these things had they almost forgot, living happy in wedlock,
Watching their children grow to strong manhood and womanhood fair;
Smoothly their lives flowed along in unbroken weal and affection,
As their devious Towy, which wound through cornland and mead to the sea.
Not a thought had the goodman of death, or of parting, than death more bitter;
But the goodwife, loving her lord, watched with solicitous thought.
Scarce from her prescient mind had faded the danger which pressed them,
The bliss which a careless touch might turn in a moment to pain;
Here on the kindly earth she had made her choice and her dwelling,

Here she would willingly live with her husband, and with him would die.
Far off her birthland appeared, cold and lifeless the mystical waters;
Better to sleep in the meads than to pass that cold portal again.
Love's light beaming warm on her life, in her veins the warm human life-blood
Filled with new longings a heart which was only half human before.
"What would life profit her now to those ice-cold abysses returning?
Better to die upon earth by the fate which awaiteth us all."
Thus the goodwife, half human in heart, mused in silence, her children around her,
Filled with a deep boding sense of the terrible nearness of fate.

Last it befell once again that the pair were bidden together
(Christening for youth, for full age bridefeasts, for old age the grave),
To a solemn burial they went; 'twas a friend of their youth who was taken.
All the desolate house was hushed in mourning and tears,
But before the dead was borne forth, the strange heart of the mystical woman,
Long keeping silence with pain, broke out at last into mirth.
Was it because she knew that the burden of living is heavy,
From what load of misery here the dead are delivered by death?
Or was it because she knew of her old primæval religion

How much higher than human life is the lot of the just who are dead?
Or was it her soul had beheld the restitution of all things,
And felt a great hope and joy which lightened the shadow of death?
Who shall tell? but her elfin nature broke forth in immoderate laughter,
Piercing the mourners' hearts, as they stood round the bier of the dead.
Long time the goodman was mute, till at last keen shame overcame him,
No more could he suffer unmoved that meaningless laughter and joy.
"Hush, hush! wife," he said, "you forget," and touched her again on the shoulder.
"For the ending of troubles I laughed," she replied, and grew grave and was still.

Then with a sob and a sigh the goodwife, looking behind her,
Rose from her place by her lord and swiftly passed forth by the door.
"Farewell," she said, "oh my love; thou hast struck me the third and the last time.
Fate 'tis that parteth us—Fate! Farewell! I shall see thee no more."
So strange she showed and so weird that the goodman dared not detain her.
Seeing his goodwife no more, and knowing the finger of Fate;
Seeing his goodwife no more, no longer the well-beloved features,
The hair that was silvered by time, the dim eyes with their motherly care;
But the radiant figure once more, golden-haired, azure-eyed, and immortal,

That at midnight arose, long ago, from the depths of the mystical lake.
None offered to stay her course, but she glided alone, unattended,
Splendid in radiant youth, up the lonely, precipitous hills.
Not to her home or her children returned, nor tarried a moment;
Straight to the hillside she went, weeping and blinded with tears,
And as she passed by the fields where her magical cattle were grazing,
Always she carolled aloud a strange and mystical song.
"Come hither, Brindle!" she sang; "come, White Spot! bring your calves with you!
Come thou, White Lord of the Herd, who wert born in the House of the King!
Come, we must go to our home! and ye, yoked patient-eyed oxen,

Come with me, come with the rest; it is time, come all
of ye home!"

The great herds heard the call, and streamed in an endless procession;
The gray oxen burst from the furrow, leaving the ploughshare behind.
Up the rough hillside they climbed behind her, obeying
her mandate,
Till they showed to the gazers below like a white cloud
mounting the steep.
Up the steep hillside they sped to the lake, and the
wondering peasants
Heard a clear voice from the hill, " Deuwch adre! Deuwch
adre! Come home!"

Never again upon earth had Rhiwallon sight of his
helpmeet,

Never again did he seek his love on the lake and the
    hills;
Wayworn and weary he grew, nor might dreams of beauty
    allure him.
The face that he loved and lost was agèd, with silvery
    hair;
But the beautiful being who went from her seat at the
    fateful banquet—
What was her youth to his age, or his age to her radiant
    youth?
What if his eyes once again should perceive the bright
    vision of old time,
Old as he was, and changed from the hopeful dreams of
    the boy?
Nay, it would kill him to see the black deep which had
    taken his life's love.
Never again did he gaze on its hateful magical face.

But the strong sons, when they knew their mother was gone from among them—

Gone without even a word, to strange death or to mystical life—

Evening by evening would climb the lonely, precipitous hillside,

Yearning if haply their eyes might see the loved features again.

Long, long vigils they spent in vain, nor ever the vision

Came, any more than it comes to all children orphaned on earth,

Till one night, when all hope was dead, they burst into passionate weeping.

"Mother, thy children," they said, "call thee, and call thee in vain.

Break through the fetters of Fate, take again thy womanly nature;

Come to us, mother, once more, let us see thee and hear thee again."

And lo! as they looked, in the moonlight a shining, beautiful figure
Came in a shallop of gold, on the silvery path of the moon.
Nearer and nearer it came; but lo! as they gazed in fond yearning,
Not as their mother it seemed, but a youthful, fairy-like form.
Gold were her locks and blue her eyes, as the clear sky of autumn.
Bitterly weeping, they turned from the lake side with sinking young hearts—
Turned from the lake side, and went, side by side, down the hill paths in silence,
Silent, with never a word, till they came within sight of their home.
Then close behind them they heard a sweet voice, which called to them softly,

And, turning round quickly, they saw the mother they loved and had lost.

"Listen, dear sons," she said. "With what spells you have drawn me ye know not.
No power but motherly love can bring an immortal to earth,
No other love can avail to reknit the bonds that are broken;
Only her child's strong cry calls back a mother again.
Give me your hands and kiss me; for see, I am old as you knew me,
The youth of those cold depths changed for the kindlier ripeness of earth.
Lo, I am now as I was, when an earthly love kept me among you,
Only I view all things with a clearer and perfecter sight.
Yours, dear sons, it must be to succour your suffering brothers.

Bound to a body which age and disease waste quickly away,
Healers your race shall be, knowing many a secret of nature,
And all the virtues of herbs, which are sent for the comfort of man.
When ye come to these lonely heights, I will meet you and speak with you always,
Teaching the secrets of life, which are hid from the great ones of earth.
Come to me often, dear sons; I shall see you afar, and will meet you,
Walk with you always, discourse with you, teach you to live and be wise.
Say to my girls that they cherish their father and comfort him always;
Bid them remember their mother, who loves as she loved them on earth.

And now, farewell, dear hearts, since to earth your yearnings have brought me.
While you live I will always be with you. Be wise, then, my children, and good."

Often at evening, the youths would climb to the mystical lake side,
Culling the simples that grew on the slopes of the desolate hills—
" Pant y Meddygon," men called it, " The dingle of the Physicians "—
And with them, wherever they went, their mother invisible came,
Teaching them all that 'tis lawful to know of the secrets of Nature
And the powers of healing that seem to be God's own prerogative gift.
Such was the knowledge they took from their loving, mystical mother,

In all our wide Britain was found no leech so skilful as they.
All the sick of the country around flocked to them to be healed by their cunning;
Broad lands in Myddfai and rank the Lord Rhys gave for their skill.
Often, for years and for years, men might see the gentle physicians
Culling the herbs on the hills, to battle with death and with pain.
From manhood to age they passed, still learning and perfecting knowledge,
Mounting the hillside at last with slower and tottering steps ;
And often a shepherd would tell of a clear voice which spoke with them always,
And oft of a shadowy form, guiding their faltering feet.

So they passed, and were laid in the grave, obeying the mandate of Nature,
Wrapt round in the sweet, cold earth by the kindly general law.
Their sons and their sons' sons came, increasing the lore of their fathers;
But no kindly Presence came to walk with them over the hills.
Slowly, through ages of Time, as the fierce glare of knowledge assails it,
Hardly the fair tale can live in the light of our commoner day;
But still through the country side runs the fame of the gentle Physicians.
The grove of Physician Evan is known in Myddfai to-day.
"Llwyn Ifan Feddyg," it runs, and another—"Llwyn Meredydd Feddyg."
Thus, in the old, old tongue, the old, old legend survives.

The skill, which through centuries lightened the burden of suffering mortals,
Lacked not memorials still in the hearts of the aged and sick;
Nay, in fair Brecknock itself, in the church of far-off Llandefallte,
Only a century since, were their praises engraved on their tombs.
Where is the sceptic would doubt the tale of the mystical mother,
If, five centuries after she went, the Meddygon of Myddfai could heal?
Or if living men in their youth, on the first fair Sabbath of August,
Have thronged from the fair town below to the banks of the mystical lake,
Hoping to see its still surface boil sudden, the white herds emerging,

And the golden shallop and oar, and the beautiful Presence of old—
Hoping, but hoping in vain, yet in simple belief unshaken,
For had they not witnessed her cures of the weak, and the halt, and the blind?

But to-day, with its broader light, flouts these beautiful stories romantic.
No more these fair visions unearthly are seen on the lakes and the hills.
From knowledge alone is power; but 'tis oh for the fair dreams of old time,
The genius which clothed deep truths in fanciful vestures and fair!
Not more in the legends of Hellas, than these fair myths of the Cymry,
Are grave truths and precious set in a beautiful framework of song.

Let them be; they are fair, they are fine, though they
    wear not their pearl on their foreheads.
Let them be; they are flowers of our Race, and as is the
    flower is the fruit.
Not in the savage tales of the Norseman the Cymry
    delighted—
Tales of blood-stained feasts and rude gods, consumed
    in a furnace of fire—
But this gentle Physician's story of ruth for suffering
    mortals,
Mild wisdom, o'ermastering Fate, young passion, and
    motherly love.
Not wholly your tale shall perish, oh kindly Physicians
    of Myddfai,
Nor the charm of that mystical soul which was born of
    and lost in the deep;
Not wholly, while speech is mine, though the low rays of
    knowledge shall flout you,

And in its broad, pitiless glare you dwindle and vanish away.

But still, as I linger and gaze, perusing the exquisite valley,
Upward by castle and peak, downward by river and town,
Whether from wooded Cystanog, or yew-shaded graves of Llangunnor,
Closing the upward gaze, far off lies the mystical steep.
Many fair scenes lie between us—gray Drysllwyn's verdant hillock,
Grongar long precious to verse, Dynevor's castle and wood,
High perched on its precipice-crags the ruins of grim Cerrigcennen,
Or the green vale higher than these, where the fair Towy winds and unwinds.

However the gaze ascends, the dark precipice closes the landscape,
Beneath whose difficult steep lies the haunted abyss of the lake.
Always the story comes back as I gaze, the beautiful legend
Which here for long ages of time the wondering peasants believed.
In yonder churchyard lie those, who ere they were freed from the body,
Grew strong through their poor brief lives by the gift of the Fair of the lake;
And, as the sun moves to the West and defines the deep shades of the hollow,
I am fired by the fair old tale, till almost I take it for true.

III.

THE CURSE OF PANTANNAS.

'MID fair Glamorgan's hills the close-set vales
Teem with men's works and toil. The great shafts rise,
Belching forth smoke and fire; the labouring beams
Of the great engines slowly rise and pause
And fall with rhythmic beat. The labouring town
Creeps down the winding valley; the poor streets
Are deep in inky dust. There comes no sound
But children's clamour or the sob or shriek
Of the quick-throbbing steam. The men are sunk
Beneath the earth, or sleeping weary sleep.
Toil, toil, or rest from toil, that is the sum
Of those unnumbered lives. Yet are they filled

With joys and griefs as are the great on earth,
And through the teeming village love and toil
Are everywhere; the poor lives come to birth
Grow ripe and are deceased, but never more
The face of nature is as 'twas at first.

But on the unfenced hillsides, far above,
The sounds, the dust, the smoke, come not at all.
Still solitude is there, where seldom foot
Of weary toil intrudes; the keen cool air
Blows fresh and still untainted on the hills;
Awhile the dark pines climb aloft, then stay,
Like a tired traveller, and naught remains
But short sweet grass and thyme and nibbling sheep,
And mountain torrents hid in deep ravines,
While the swift gaze ranges from vale to vale
Masked by its veil of smoke. And, when 'tis night,
Immense Auroras, glaring o'er the sky,

Mark where amid the folded hillsides lies
The City of the Martyr. Here, where still
The Cymric lore, the Cymric speech survive,
The half-forgotten fables of old time,
Of gnome and fairy, flourish undisturbed
Amid the noontide glare of common day,
And one there is reaped from this very spot
And breathing of the race, and it is this :—

———

Long, long ago, the fair-folk on the earth
Were frequent, and their rings upon the meads
Showed green wherever virgin pastures were,
And o'er the leas their elfin music thrilled
Whether of oaten pipe or silvery flute,
While the young moon was rising on the hills,
And the gay elves footed it merrily

The Curse of Pantannas.

Upon the dry smooth turf. So oft they came,
Summer and winter, on his sweet short grass,
That one grave churl who at Pantannas dwelt,
Hating the senseless revel and the race,
In anger to the witch who dwelt hard by
Revealed his case, demanding if she knew
Some potent charm wherewith to free his life
From this insensate mirth of godless souls.
Then she, knowing his wish and all the lore
Of the forbidden books, counselled him thus :—

" Wherever on thy pastures shows a ring
Which tells of elfin revelry by night,
Yoke thy strong oxen, driving straight through them
Thy ploughs, till all lie fallow. Sow them thick
With kindly corn fit for the use of man,
So, when the harvest comes, this tricksy folk,
That hates the newer race of mortal men

And that which gives them food, will come no more,
For chiefly the unsullied meads they love
Where never ploughshare came since the old time
Ere men were first on earth. So shalt thou gain
Great harvests for thy wealth, and shalt disperse
This cursèd people, and shalt reap thy land
Till all thy barns o'erflow, and thou indeed
Art lord of thy own lands far more than now.
Do thou this thing, and Fortune shall be thine,
And peace and the full mastery of thy own."

So did the churl. He drove his iron ploughs
Through the inviolate meads, and straight the sounds
Of dance and song grew silent. Never more
Came those strange elfin rings upon his fields,
Nor any traveller passing saw a glimpse
Of those quick-tripping feet ; but far away
The fair-folk turned, where yet no cruel share

Was sent to kill the greensward. Springtide came :
The fields grew splendid with the wheat's bright green,
When, one day as the sun had kissed the hills,
The grave churl, turning homeward, saw a form
Upon his path which threatened him, and said,
" Daw dial ! " " Vengeance comes ! " And in the night,
When all was still, there came a noise which shook
The house as though 'twould fall, and the same voice,
" Daw dial ! " And when now 'twas harvest-tide
And the great barns stood open for the grain,
One night, no ear nor straw was in the fields,
Only black ashes, and the same strange form
Met him again, pointing a sword at him,
And in the same weird accents " It begins,"
" Nid yw ond dechreu."
                      Then the churl, afraid,
Begged for forgiveness, willing that the fields
Should turn to meads again, whereon the sprite

Promised at last that he would pray his king
Forgiveness of the fault, and come again
On the third day, bringing his lord's behest.

   Now, when the third day came, the churl went forth
Through his burnt fields, and there again the elf
Waited, and to the other made report,
" The king's word is for aye unchangeable,
And vengeance must be done. Still, since thy fault
Thou dost repent, and hast atoned in part,
Therefore, not in thy time, nor of thy sons,
Shall the curse fall, but, poised on high, await
Thy distant seed." Then he, as one who hears
Reprieve from death, o'erjoyed sent forth his hinds
To turn the corn to pasture. Once again
The dark green rings grew frequent on the grass,
The gay elves danced, the old melodious sounds
Of song and music gladdened all the fields,

And he grew rich and passed in peaceful age,
And his sons followed him, and slept in peace.

   But still, when fourscore years or more had fled,
The dread voice came at times, repeating still
The self-same threat, " Daw dial ! " " Vengeance comes ! "
Oft heard across the years ; but since long use
Obscures the sense, so, when this warning came
And no harm followed it, the wealthy squire
Who held Pantannas then, took little heed
Of half-forgotten memories. His young son
Rhydderch was come to manhood, and would wed
Gwen, daughter of Pencraig, and both their houses
Were fain of it. A noble pair were they,
In fitted years, and rank, and mutual troth.
No cloud came on the sky of their young love,
But all men praised the bridegroom's gallant port
And the bride's sweetness, and they made a feast

At gray Pantannas ere the marriage day,
Whereto the fair girl Gwen and all her kin
Were bidden.   It was the wintry joyous time
Of Yuletide and the birth-time of the Lord,
When all hearts, for the sacred season glad,
Make merry in the fading of the year.

With mirth had sped the feast; all round the hearth
Were seated, Gwen and Rhydderch side by side.
Careless they winged the hours with tale and song.
The night was still, there came no breath of sound,
Only without the loud unceasing fall
Of the full river plunging down the rocks,
Only within the noise of mirth and song.

Then suddenly they seemed to hear a voice
Above the roaring stream.   A silence fell
On all the joyous group.   Not as the voice

The Curse of Pantannas.

So often heard it came, but seemed to wail
Some unremembered word. The maiden clung
Close to her lover for a while, and then
The jovial hearth, the jest, the tale, the song,
Chased all their fears, and all was as before.
No sound without but the unceasing noise
Of the full river plunging down the rocks.

Then, swift again, above the sounds of mirth,
Above the river roaring through the rocks,
A clear voice, dreadful, pealed, "The Time is come!"
"Daeth Amser!" thus it wailed. And all the guests
Rose to the door, seeking whence came the voice,
And first the goodman went, his worn cheek pale
With fear, remembering the tales he heard
In boyhood of the voice. Long time they stood
Expecting, but no voice they heard, nor sound,
But the loud river plunging down the rocks.

Till, as they turned them houseward once again,
Above the roaring waters, three times heard,
The same voice pealed, "The Time is come! the Time!"
Then they affrighted and in silence went
Within the house, and then a mighty noise
Crashed round them, and it seemed a mighty hand
Shook all to the foundations. As they sate
In fear, without a word, a shapeless hag
Stood at the casement. Then one, bolder, said,
"Why comest thou, thou loathely thing?" And she,
"Peace, chatterer, I have naught with thee. I come
To tell the doom which waits this cursed house
And that which weds with it. But since thy tongue
Is thus injurious, never will I lift
The veil that doth conceal it." With the word
She vanished, none knew whither.
                                When she had gone,
And all was still again, the cry, the cry,

Rose loud and ceased not. Then a deep affright
Fell upon all, and gloom. The hour grew late,
And from the hapless house the trembling guests
Went on their lonely ways. Rhydderch alone,
Grown careless in the flush of innocent love,
Delayed his love's departure, till they went
Alone at midnight down the haunted vale,
Across the roaring waters. Unafraid
The lovers fared, nor voice nor shape of ill
Assailed them, undismayed, defying all
The unseen powers of Death and Doom and Ill,
Strong in the virgin mail of mutual love.

But when the maid was safe within her home,
And it was time to part, some livelier sense
Of peril took her, and her boding fear
Burst forth in tender words. "Dearest," she said,
"Good-night! Farewell! Some sense of coming ill

Weighs down my heart. If we should meet no more,
Or if some long delay should cheat our love,
I will be faithful always, and will wed
With thee, and none beside. Ay, though the powers
Of ill should part us all our lives and leave me
Widowed of thee!" And he, " Fear not, my life,
The Power of Love protects us. If I come not
At once to claim thee, as indeed I hope,
And if the powers of ill have might to part
Our lives awhile, yet am I true to thee.
It may be some dark ruin waits our house
For some forgotten wrong; yet, what care I?
They cannot touch our lives, these envious powers,
Nor blight our love. What care I for the rest,
My treasure, having thee?"

                              Then, with a kiss,
They parted unafraid, and the youth passed
The ceaseless voices and the roaring stream

Undaunted, clothed with love, and caring naught
For things of earth or air.
                            But as he sped
Across the self-same fields, which long years past
The ploughshare broke, hard by some haunted cave
Beneath the hill, a ring of fairy green
Before him showed, around him bursts of mirth
Came of invisible throats, and silvery sounds
Of elfin music sweet; and, rapt in love,
And thinking careless of his dear alone,
He stepped within the circle, and was lost,
While Time should last, to home, and kin, and love.

  For nowhere might his sorrowing parents find
Trace of their son. They searched the country round,
Through every grove and brake; they searched the
      depths
Of the loud plunging stream; but never at all

They found him. Then, when many weeks had gone,
They sought a hermit in his holy cell,
And told him all, the wailing cry which rang
Through the sad night, the loathely form which came.
They told him all, and he, with grief and tears,
Knowing what judgment must o'ertake the youth,
Though guiltless, bade the mourners hope no more
To see him, whether in life he was or death;
And they, lamenting him as lost, at last
Lived their old life, and all was as before,
Till, losing not their sorrow, but bent down
By weight of time, they passed, and in the ground
Were laid, but never again beheld their son.

But Gwen, the gentle maiden, when she knew
That which had been, and how her love was gone,
Mourned for him long, and long time would lament
The cruelty of fate, but never at all

Believed that he was dead, for still she held
That he would come again—it might be soon,
It might be after years, but still would come,
As his word promised. So she dried her tears,
Feeding a deathless hope, and every day,
Morning and evening, when the circling sun
Burst from the gates of dawn, or sank in night,
Upon the summit of the scarpèd rock
Would stand, and scan the landscape far and near,
Seeking her love's return, and, when he came not,
Descend in grief. Year after year she came,
Till from love's casements her unfaltering soul
Looked dimly, and the gathering snows of time
Whitened her chestnut locks, yet still she came,
Steadfast, nor failed of hope, while yet she could,
Still looking for her love. Until, at last,
By the old chapel of the Van, they laid
Her mortal body and undying hope.

The years slipped by, the undelaying years,
And one by one they passed, the young and old
Who knew the story; scarcely one was left
To tell of Rhydderch or his fate; the world
Rolled round upon its course; young lives were born,
Grew ripe, and faded; many a youth and maid
Came careless, rapt in love, and read the stone
Which told of Gwen, nor knew what powers of ill
Blighted her life and hope, for never more
The elfin music sounded on the leas
Since that dread night of Yule. Another race,
With other hopes and fears, was on the earth,
And the old vanished hopes, and fears, and loves,
Were gone, clean gone, like mist upon the hills.

*   *   *   *   *

Then, one fair summer morning, from the cave
Where, on that sad night four score years ago,

His footsteps strayed, Rhydderch came forth again
In all the pride of youth. His heart beat high
With love and hope, nor felt he any change,
More than he feels, who, a brief month or more,
Leaves his loved home. His longing heart was full;
He listened to the joyous notes of song
Which the gay thrushes sang, as when he went
To meet his love. Slow Nature showed no change,
The old oaks seemed the same, his sweetheart's home
The same, or hardly changed. The bitter Past
Touched him no more, who for the Future looked
And recompense of love. There were the graves
Beneath the yew, where he in happy tryst
Had lingered with his love when moonrise came,
As soon he should again. "He had been ill,
Entranced, and the good folk who tended him,
He knew not where, made light of the long weeks
Which lay 'tween him and health. When he was there

"Twas Yule-tide, now 'twas May." He raised his eyes
To see if there, where then it used to wait,
A girl's form waited. Something grey was there,
Half-hidden beneath the yew. Was it herself?
He vaulted o'er the wall, and found—a stone
Grey touched by time, and graven on it deep
In words half-hid by lichen, the sweet name
Of her he loved, "Died, aged threescore years,"
And in some strange year, forty years to come.

Then not so much a sense of grief and pain
Took him as fear. He knew not what had been;
He knew not what he was. His throbbing pulse
Grew slower at the chill cold touch of fate,
And great perplexity and new-born doubt,
And some half-consciousness of long-dead years,
As of a dream, enchained him. Soon he thought
The mists would vanish, leaving all things clear,

The Curse of Pantannas.

And then the love, the passion of his youth
Once more would live again. So, eagerly
He left the place of graves, and took his way
Along the well-known paths, to where he saw,
In the old spot—the same, yet not the same—
The roof-tree of Pantannas. Not as yet
Had he seen human face, and a new fear
Came on him, and strange shame, as of one come
From other air than earth's; for now he knew
That either he was dazed and weak of brain,
Or some great change had passed upon his life,
Which nothing but the gaze of human eyes
And the remembered tones of human speech
Might ever again dispel. And so he went
Up the old path, and gained the well-known door,
And in the old room stood again and mused,
Changed—yet the same; but human face or voice
He saw not. All the people were afield,

Nor was there any there to see or hear
Of those he knew of old.   Then, when the load
Of silence grew too great, through the still house,
In his high youthful voice, he called for one,
His childish serving boy, who always loved
To follow him, whether with horse or hound,
All day upon the hills, "Ifan, 'tis I,
I have come back, 'Deuwch yma.'"   The high voice
Through the void space resounding clear, at last
Echoed to where, within a sunny nook,
Bent double with the weight of ninety years,
There dozed an agèd man, half deaf, half blind,
And when he heard, his limbs began to shake,
And he to mutter to himself; again
It came, the old man trembled to his feet;
The third time came the cry, and then in haste,
Tottering, the aged figure, bowed and bent,
Moved quickly to the door, and there beheld

His long-lost master, fair in youthful bloom,
Unchanged, and in his habit as he was
When all the world was young.
                            The old man's heart
Went out to him, who stood unmoved, untouched,
Not knowing whom he saw.   One word alone
He uttered, " Rhydderch."
                            And with a flash of light
The Past revealed itself.   The youth knew all
That had been, reading in another's face
The unnoted flight of Time.   His life was done;
He knew it now.   All his old longings dead;
Dust was his love, and all his yearnings dust;
Dust was his life, and all his body dust.
No more upon the old earth could he bear
To walk amid the light of garish day,
And when the white-haired man, with tears of joy,
Would fain have kissed his hand, the Life in Death

Shrank from the Death in Life, and fading, left
Naught but a thin dust, lost in empty air.

Thus side by side they move, the Lives of Toil
And Fancy. What is Fancy but the Past
Or Future, bathed in light which never shone,
Or shall, upon the earth, and yet which shows
Nearer than real Life, and clearer far—
A Life wherein the terror of the world,
Its mystery, its awe, its boundless hope,
Are plainer than in ours, wherein the pang
Of hopeless longing and unmerited pain
Which vex our thought, the blind unequal lot
Which takes us, find some vague apology,
And hope some dim fulfilment, and the ways
Of Fate are justified, the righteous rise,
The wicked fall? Die not, oh sacred star

Of Fancy. Show us still the charm, the awe,
The glamour of our lives, bitterer griefs,
Joys keener than our own ; loftier heights,
Depths deeper still : keep mystery, which is
The nurse of knowledge, shading from the glare
Of the full noontide sun, our tree of Life.

TO A GAY COMPANY.

A GRASSY little knoll I know,
Before the windows of my home,
Where, when the chill days longer grow,
And the slow Spring has come,

Forth gleams a golden company
Of lowly blossoms through the grass,
Smiling a welcome back to me
As the soft Spring days pass.

Daily they take the cloudless sun;
With innocent faces free from guile,
And a sweet yearning never done,
They look on him and smile.

To a Gay Company.

And while he shines, the livelong day,
From early morn to failing light,
Stands patiently the dense array,
Content and smiling bright.

But if cold rain or wintry hail
Touch them, the careful petals fold,
Safe where no violence may assail
Their shining cups of gold.

Oh, silent, innocent choir! I seem
To hear your fairy voices rise,
Extolling faint, as in a dream,
Your great Lord in the skies;

And read in your wide-opened eyes
Strange thoughts and human histories,
Till from your humble lives seems grown
Life fairer than your own.

Fair celandines, I love to see
Each year your radiant company
Bloom golden on the springing grass,
As the quick seasons pass.

No careless foot shall come to mar
Your peaceful lives, while life is mine;
Still as the Spring-tide comes shall shine
Each multitudinous star,

So like the others, and the dead
Dear blossoms of forgotten Mays,
The joyous Springs which now are fled,
The wondering childish days

When you, a joyous company,
Or yours, were of an age with me;
When marvels filled the earth and sky,
Nor you could fade, nor I.

To a Gay Company.

Still shall I seem to hear your voice
Of joyous praise, though all be still;
The Spring-time, bidding all rejoice,
Through you and me shall thrill.

Whether we be alive on earth,
Or lying hidden in the mould,
The Spring shall come with throes of birth,
And clothe the fields with gold.

And me, whom the same Maker made,
Shall no renewal touch? Shall I
Beyond all hope decay and fade?
Deeper than Spring-tide lie?

Nay, nay! the sun shines overhead,
The Spring-tide calls, the winter's done;
At last, from close depths dark and dead,
I, too, shall greet the Sun.

FROM JUVENAL.

I READ to-day a Poet dead
    In old Rome, centuries ago;
Once more returned the days long fled,
    The dried-up waters seemed to flow.

Once more the keen tongue known in youth
    Lashed the gross vices of the time,
Portraying with a dreadful truth
    The sloughs of sense, the deeps of crime.

Great city of the World! were these
    All that the race has gained of thee—
Foul lusts and soulless luxuries,
    Fraud, bloodshed, depths of villany?

From Juvenal.

Was this what we have left of Rome,
  This blood-stained sink of dark offence?
Nay, still across the ages come
  The high pure tones of innocence:

"Let nothing ever, base to see or hear,
  Pass the chaste threshold where a young soul is;
The innocence of boyhood, oh, revere,
  Lest what of vileness you conceive be his.

"Despise not thou his pure and tender youth,
  But let his weakness stand 'twixt thee and wrong."
Not wholly wert thou dumb, dread voice of Truth!
  Nor lost, oh sacred ministry of Song!

IGHTHAM MOTE.

The gray house from the moat around
Rises four-square; two white swans glide;
A falling stream's uncertain sound
Is heard on every side.

A home in an untroubled land,
As 'twas at first it is to-day;
Unchanged the grey quadrangles stand,
Through centuries past away.

The drawbridge and the entrance tower
Are still as in those good old days,
Ere freedom baffled lawless power,
Which dullards love to praise.

Ightham Mote.

So old, so grey, so ripe with time—
Ere the old cedars on the grass
Came from some new-discovered clime
It saw the centuries pass.

So old and yet so new; to-day
Flowers of Japan, in gold and white,
Its builders dreamt not of, make bright
Its gradual decay.

And rounding into leafy bowers
The laurustinus' bulk is spread;
A tall tree bending overhead
Its delicate wealth of flowers.

And over every moss-grown stone
A glamour of the dead is cast—
The charm of days deceased and done,
The phantoms of the Past.

Songs of Britain.

A home, a hundred homes in one,
Before our English race grew great,
Before the doughty deeds were done
Which fixed her glorious fate;

Before the dauntless Buccaneer
From Devon dared the western seas,
And drove the sullen Don in fear,
And robbed his argosies;

Before the White Rose and the Red,
Ere Crecy proved our England's might,
When scarce the Paynim learnt to dread
The steel-clad Northern knight.

A hundred tales of good and ill,
Of love and right, of hate and wrong,
The joyance and the dole which fill
The treasure-house of song.

Ightham Mote.

The old knights with their mail were here,
The dames demure with high-built hair,
The grave ruffed sage, the cavalier
Flaunting his lovelocks fair,

The periwigged and powdered Beau,
The Dame with hoops and patches brave;
The generations come and go—
The cradle and the grave.

Our grandsires and our granddames came;
They came awhile, their times are dead,
And we, the modern sir and dame,
Are reigning in their stead.

Unchanged the old grange stands, and will
When we in turn are past and gone;
The hurrying years flit by us still,
Life glides unnoticed on.

And what the end? No Goth or Hun
Can blot the record of thy past;
Shalt thou, unchanged, untroubled, last
Till history be done?

The peasants spared thee, the long shock
Of warring Roses came not near;
The Roundhead and the Cavalier,
The King's head on the block,

Thou hast survived. Shall peace o'erturn
What banded foemen deigned to spare,
In some deep hate, when all things fair
In one red ruin burn?

Or shall a wider faith and trust
Bind all, until men recognize
No good but mutual sacrifice,
Nor aim but to be just?

Ightham Mote.

Thou liest within the net of Fate,
Oh ancient England of our love!
Howe'er the circling world may move.
Thou art, thou hast been great!

THE SECRET OF THINGS.

Did the Race of men descend from a Nature sublime,
    From a type which is higher than man and almost divine,
Sinking from higher to lower through æons of time,
    Through a hopeless decay and slow unmeasured decline?

Whence came, then, this downward force to degrade what God gave?
    Can we rest in the thought that we fell from a higher estate?
Shall the work of His hand grow weaker in time and fade,
    And that which was once above death, sink down to the grave?

And if we are born with the seeds of a deep decay,
　　Can it ever be stayed, though it were by an Infinite Will;
Or are all things fated to fade and diminish away
　　Through all stages of lower life till Creation lies still?

Or if power there be to stay, and willing for good,
　　Where then shall be set the limit of gradual shame?
Not there, maybe, where we think, nor then when we would,
　　And how shall our being reascend to the height whence we came?

Or shall this faith rather be ours, that the Infinite Plan
　　Is worked by a gradual miracle bettering the Race,
Since the quickening Spirit breathed on the sea's dead face,
　　And the faint life stirred, which one day should blossom in Man?

It were liker, indeed, to the work of an Infinite Might
    To raise all the gradual Past from lower to higher;
Nay, but where, were it thus, were there room for the heaven-sent light
    That, 'midst growing darkness shining, could bid us aspire?

And what were our profit to rise from the general shame,
    If we knew that the Race were doomed to a deeper decay,
Or if millions of lives that are past should wither in flame,
    Nor rise from the darkness of Hell to a Heavenly day?

And does not all Nature teem, not only with types that ascend,
    But with those their ineffable fates from a higher ideal degrade,

High archetypes dwindling down, which from higher to lower tend,
    Keen organs, and powers of might, which to feeble energies fade?

Great Universe, what is thy Secret, what are thy Laws?
    Do they dwindle through secular time by the power of an Infinite Will?
Or do all things to Perfectness tend by a changeless ordinance still,
    Impelled by the upward force of an inborn Beneficent Cause?

But if such were the law of things, how then should any ignore
    The self-same embryo growth of man and the lowest ape,

Which an inborn necessity moulds to such difference of
    being and shape,
  That one rises to godlike discourse, one lies soulless
    for evermore?

Or shall we believe, indeed, that deep down in the
    covering earth
  May be found, some day, a trace of a Being that once
    has been,
Which in long dead æons of time was parent of either
    birth,
  And, in Nature's gradual scheme, stood centred and
    fixed between?

Can the Individual rise, though the Race sinks down in
    disgrace,
  And, while all is ruined beside, increase to a heavenly
    height?

Can the Individual sink to some dark, ineffable place,
　　While the Race rises higher and higher in face of the
　　　　Infinite Light?

Is the soul of Humanity one with the Individual soul?
　　Shall each rise with the other or sink, as the suns are
　　　　illumined or fade?
Shall the hand of the Maker show weak as the æons
　　unchangeably roll,
　　Grown helpless to stay the wreck of the Cosmos itself
　　　　hath made?

Nay, from out of the House of despair shall be heard a
　　jubilant voice,
　　Beneath the deepest depths and hopeless abysses of Ill,
Which in cosmical accents immense, bids all things living
　　rejoice,
　　And out of the pit of Hell strive onward and upward still.

OH, EARTH!

Oh, earth! that liest still to-night
   Beneath the starlit skies,
How splendid dost thou loom and bright
   To planetary eyes!

But if some storm-cloud, vast and dark,
   Should hide thee from the day;
If through blind night no faintest spark
   Should force its feeble way,

No other would thy face appear,
   Than on this cloudless sky,
Though all the world should quake with fear,
   Though all our race should die.

Oh, Earth!

Great Universe! too vast thou art,
   Too changeless and too far,
Dull grows the brain and chill the heart
   Before the nearest star.

Oh, kindly earth! upon thy breast
   For ever let me lie,
Wrapt round with thy eternal rest,
   But gazing on the sky.

ON A BIRTHDAY.

What shall be written of the man
   Who through life's mingled hopes and fears
Touches to-day our little span
   Of seventy years;

Who, with force undiminished still,
   A Nestor stands among his peers,
Full of youth's fire and dauntless will
   At seventy years;

Who knows no creeping chill of age,
   But, rich in all which life endears,
Keeps still the patriot's noble rage
   Through seventy years,

On a Birthday.

The form unbent, the flashing eye,
    The curious lore, the wit that cheers,
The scorn of wrong which can defy
    His seventy years;

To whom no wound which mars the state,
    No humblest neighbour's grief or tears,
Appeal in vain for love or hate
    These seventy years;

For whom home's happy radiance yet
    A steadfast beacon-fire appears,
Bright through the storms, the stress, the fret
    Of seventy years;—

What else but this? "Brave heart, be strong,
    Be of good hope; life holds no fears,
Nor death, for him who strives with wrong
    For seventy years.

Live, labour, spread that sacred light
    Of knowledge which thy soul reveres;
Fight still the old victorious fight
    Of seventy years.

Live, labour, ripen to fourscore
    While still the listening Senate hears;
Live till new summers blossom o'er
    These seventy years.

Or if a brighter briefer lot
    Withdraw thee from thy country's tears,
Be sure there is where change is not,
    Nor age, nor years."

IN A GERMAN LABORATORY.

A most intelligent dog I took,
Affectionate, full of caressing grace,
With something of human love in his look,
And such a trustful, half-human face.

Had learnt tricks, too—would give you a paw
Where a brother-man would offer a hand,
Right or left, as you asked him; could understand
Your speech—it might almost fill one with awe,

Seeing how near to mankind, yet how far
These dumb and pitiful creatures are;
How all their faith and belief and love
Is centred in Man as a Lord above.

And looking into his eyes for awhile,
For knowledge is precious and gained through pain,
I bound him down with a pitying smile,
And deftly removed the left lobe of his brain.

And then, with all that I had of skill,
I healed it again, so that presently,
Though lame and sick, in his love for me,
The creature strove to obey my will.

And when I asked him to give me a paw,
He gave the left first, but when for the right
I asked, his maimed brain failing him quite,
Gave the left—and I thought I had touched on a Law.

So I persevered, and the brute again,
With a loving, sorrowful look of pain,
Brought the left paw over the helpless right,
And I marked the effort, with deep delight.

In a German Laboratory.

And having pushed knowledge so far, again
I divided the opposite lobe of the brain,
And the poor brute, though willing to offer a paw,
Could no longer obey—and I grasped a Law.

Later on, still athirst for knowledge, once more
I carved the weak brain, as I did before,
Till the poor dumb wretch, as he lay on his side,
With a loving look regarding me, died.

Poor brute! he lies dead for knowledge, and I,
If I grasp not the clue, yet I may by-and-by.
Strange how weak Man is, and infirm of will,
For sometimes I see him and shudder still!

THE SUMMONS.

MARCH 28, 1884.

Away from love of child and wife,
From the first flush of ripening life,
From books and Art, from all things fair,
From homely joys, from public care,
A low voice summons us away,
And prince and peasant must obey.

Sometimes amid the noonday throng,
Amid the feast, the dance, the song,
Amid the daily wholesome round,
The inevitable accents sound,
And the ear hears the summons come
As his who calls a truant home.

The Summons.

And sometimes in the lonely night
It sounds and brings with it the light.
Alone, with none but strangers nigh,
Comes the cold voice which bids us die ;
Sudden, or after months of pain,
And weary vigils spent in vain.

What shall it bring of profit then
To have loomed large in the eyes of men ?
Or what of comfort shall endure,
Save soaring thoughts and memories pure ?
Nought else of thoughts and things that be
Can solace that great misery.

Oh dreadful summons, full of fear
For weakling mortal souls to hear !
When that last moment shall be ours,
'Mid failing brain and sinking powers,
May one great strength our steps attend,
The constant presence of a Friend.

SILVERN SPEECH.

There are whom Fate's obscure decree
Dooms in deep solitude to be;
For whom no word that mortal spake
The sullen silence comes to break;
And e'en the music of the Spheres
Falls only on unheeding ears.
For them, life's loud processions seem
A noiseless and unmeaning dream.
Around their prison, joyous life
Echoes with noise of fruitful strife.
Yet, to their cells no sound may come,
But all the universe is dumb.
Ah! strange that while all things rejoice

Silvern Speech.

Man only should be wanting voice!
Ah! strange that morning-song of bird
By living ears is never heard!
Nor mighty master-music dim,
Nor Heaven-thrilled note of soaring hymn,
Nor rippling laugh of happy child,
Nor the Deep's thunder-voices wild!
Unreached by life's tumultuous sound
Even as the dead, beneath the ground.
And still, though all creation groan,
Unmoved in loneliness alone.
Ah, cruel fate! unequal doom
That sinks the innocent in gloom!
What first the depths of chaos stirred
But the Ineffable Spoken Word?
What else our inmost souls can reach
Like that Divinest Gift of Speech?
Ah, hapless fate that thus deprives
Of half their life unconscious lives!

Ah! could a soft compassion gain
To soothe the victims' lonely pain!

What if with knowledge, love combined,
Can wake the undeveloped mind,
And without speech or sound can teach
The use of sound alike and speech;
To those dumb solitudes profound
Convey some blessed ghost of sound,
And kindle from the dormant sense
Bright sparks of new intelligence;
Assist the undeveloped brain
New loftier summits to attain,
Till knowledge grow the guide of love,
And love turned Heavenward point above:
And the illumined soul confess
The innate love of Righteousness!
Surely a miracle it is
Which works so blest a change as this!

THE OBELISK.

Upon the river side,
   Above the turbid stream,
Which rolls on, deep and wide ;
   Strange as a dream,

The obelisk defies
   Its dim unnumbered years,
Facing the murky skies,
   Their snows, their tears.

Three thousand years it stood
   Upon the sweet, broad Nile,
And watched the gliding flood,
   The blue skies smile.

Songs of Britain.

And many a century more,
    Where it of old would stand,
It lay half covered o'er
    By the hot sand.

Now with signs graven deep,
    In this our Northern Isle,
Where the skies often weep
    And seldom smile,

Once more again it rears
    Its dim, discrownèd head,
Though all those countless years
    Its life is dead.

Forgotten is the lore
    Its mystic symbols keep ;
Its builders evermore
    Sleep their last sleep.

The Obelisk.

Amid this Northern air,
    Beyond the storm-tost sea,
Where earth nor sky is fair,
    Why shouldst thou be?

Standing amidst the strife,
    The modern city's roar,
Memorial of a life
    Dead evermore,

And of the end of all
    That shows to-day so strong,
The greatness that shall fall,
    After how long?

The city which to-day
    Shows mightier than thy own,
Which yet shall pass away,
    Like thine o'erthrown.

And thou? Where shalt thou be
    When Time has ruined all,
And Faith and Empery
    Together fall?

Shalt thou at last find rest
    Beneath the river's flow,
And mark upon its breast
    New ages grow?

Or shall some unborn race
    Take thee as prize of war,
And set thee up to grace
    New cities far?

Or shall our Northern frost,
    Our chill and weeping skies,
Sap thee, till thou art lost
    To mortal eyes?

The Obelisk.

The Past it is, the Past
   Whose ghost thou comest here;
The years fleet by us fast,
   The end draws near.

But while the Present flies
   The far-off Past survives;
It lives, it never dies,
   In newborn lives.

It lives, it never dies,
   And we the outcome are
Of countless centuries
   And ages far.

What if our thought might see
   The Future ere it rise,
The ages that shall be,
   Before our eyes;

And if incorporate,
    Graven by some mystic hand,
Our hieroglyph of Fate
    By thine might stand?

Nay, nay, our Future shows
    Implicitly in thee;
For well the thinker knows
    What was, shall be.

And though a ghost thou art,
    'Tis well that thou art here
To touch each careless heart
    With hope and fear.

A SONG OF EMPIRE.

June 20, 1887.

First Lady of our English race,

In Royal dignity and grace

Higher than all in old ancestral blood,

But higher still in love of good,

And care for ordered Freedom, grown

To a great tree where'er

In either hemisphere,

Its vital seeds are blown;

Where'er with every day begun

Thy English bugles greet the coming sun!

Thy life is England's. All these fifty years
Thou from thy lonely Queenly place
Hast watched the clouds and sunshine on her face;
Hast marked her changing hopes and fears;
Her joys and sorrows have been always thine;
Always thy quick and Royal sympathy
Has gone out swiftly to the humblest home,
Wherever grief and pain and suffering come.

Therefore it is that we
Take thee for head and symbol of our name.
For fifty years of reign thou wert the same,
Therefore to-day we make our jubilee.
Firm set on ancient right, as on thy people's love,
Unchecked thy wheels of empire onward move.
Not as theirs is thy throne
Who, though their hapless subjects groan,
Sit selfish, caring not at all,

Until the fierce mob surges and they fall,
Or the assassin sets the down-trod free.
Not such thy fate on this thy jubilee,
But love and reverence in the hearts of all.

Oh England! Empire wide and great
As ever from the shaping hand of fate
Did issue on the earth, august, large grown!
What were the Empires of the past to thine,
The old old Empires ruled by kings divine—
Egypt, Assyria, Rome? What rule was like thine own,
Who over all the round world bearest sway?
Not those alone who thy commands obey
Thy subjects are; but in the boundless West
Our grandsires lost, still is thy reign confest.
"The Queen" they call thee, the young People strong,
Who, being Britons, might not suffer wrong,
But are reknit with us in reverence for thee;
Therefore it is we make our jubilee.

See what a glorious throng they come,
Turned to their ancient home,
The children of our England! See
What vigorous company
Thou sendest, Greater England of the Southern Sea!
Thy stately cities, thick with domes and spires,
Chase the illumined night with festal fires
In honour of their Queen, whose happy reign
Began when, 'mid their central roar,
The naked savage trod the pathless plain.
Thousands of miles, North, South, East, West, to-day,
Their countless herds and flocks unnumbered stray.
Theirs are the vast primæval forest depths profound;
Yet everywhere are found
The English laws, the English accents fair,
'Mid burning North or cooler Southern air.
A world within themselves, and with them blent
Island with continent

The green isles, jewels on the tropic blue,
Where flower and tree and bird are strange and new:
Or that which lies within a temperate air
As summer-England fair;
Or those, our Southern Britain that shall be,
Set in the lonely sea.
Lands of deep fiord and snow-clad soaring hill,
Wherethrough the ocean-currents ebb and fill,
And craters vast, wherefrom the prisoned force
Of the great earth-fires runs its dreadful course.
And vales of fern and palm, whence rising like a dream
High in mid-heaven, the ghostly ice-fields gleam.

And from her far and wintry North
The great Dominion issues forth,
Fit nurse of stalwart British hearts and strong;
From her black pine woods, deep in snow,

Her billowy prairies boundless as the sea,
Where on the sweet untroubled soil
Yearly the unnoticed, countless wild-flowers blow,
And by men's fruitful and compelling toil
Yearly the deep and bounteous harvests grow;
From the lone plains, wherethrough the icy wind
Sweeps from the North, leaving the Pole behind;
In whose brief summer suns, so fierce they shine,
Flourish alike the apple and the vine;
From teeming ancient cities bright and fair,
Whether in summer's heat or frosty wintry air,
Stamped with the nameless charm and grace
Of a more joyous race;
Or on the rounding prairie nestling down
Homestead and frequent new-built town.
Even to those ultimate wilds where comes to be
Another Westminster on the Pacific Sea.

Nor shall thy Western Isles
Be wanting, where the high green breakers fall
Upon the torrid shore, and nature smiles;
And yet sometimes broods over all,
Thick woods and hot lagunes with steaming breath,
A nameless presence with a face of death.
Fair balmy Isles, where never wintry air
Ruffles the scentless tropic blossoms fair,
Upon whose sun-warmed fruitful soil
Our father's dusky freedmen toil.
Lands of bright plumes that flash from tree to tree,
Long creepers trailing thick with brilliant bloom,
And loud upon the forest's silent gloom
The plunging surges of the encircling sea.

And from the ancient land
Scorching beneath the strong unfailing sun,
Round thee thy unnumbered subject millions stand;

From many a storied city fair,
Old ere our England, first begun,
From marble tomb and temple white,
Built ere our far forefathers were,
And still a miracle defying Time;
Palaces gray with age and dark with crime,
Fierce superstitions, only quenched in blood,
And sweet flower-fancies yearning towards the light,
And lustral cleansings in the sacred flood,
Where by dim temple cool, or shaded street,
From hill or parchèd plain the wayworn pilgrims meet.

And from the unhappy Continent
Which breeds the savage and the slave—
From our enormous South, there shall be sent
A scanty band of strong self-governed men.
And from those poisoned swamps, to-day a grave,
But which one day shall smile with plenty, when

A Song of Empire.

The onward foot of Knowledge, slow, sublime,
Has traversed her and set her children free
From ocean to her fabulous inland sea,
And the fierce savage, full of kingly grace,
Is father of a gentler race,
And peaceful commerce heals the wounds of Time,
And the long history of blood and pain
Comes nevermore again.

And nearest to thee, and of all most dear,
Thy people of these little Northern Isles,
Who never shall their Queen forget,
Nor be forgotten, whether Fortune smiles
Or armèd Europe storm around,
Whom none assail, beyond the waves' deep sound,
Behind their surge-struck ramparts safe and free
These are thy closest subjects, these
The brain and heart of Empire, as thy Rose

Within its close-ranged petals comes to hold
A perfumed heart of gold,
Wherein the seed of the miraculous flower,
Safe hid, defies Fate's power.
And most of all thy wondrous mother-town
Upon our broad Thames sitting like a crown,
Who, 'mid her healthful labour-laden air,
Grows every day more fair;
Whom not for fairness do her children prize,
But for her gracious homely memories—
A nation, not a city, the loved home
Whereto the longing thoughts of exiled Britons come!

   What is it that their voices tell?
What is it that in naming thee they praise?
Not wider empire only; that is well.
But there are worthier triumphs, peaceful days,
Just laws, a people happier than before,

A Song of Empire.

And rolling on untroubled evermore,
With larger stream, and fuller and more free
The tide of ordered liberty.
These things than empire higher are,
Higher and nobler far.

   Our old Draconic Law
With children's blood cemented, no more kills
Its tale of innocent victims.   Pitying Love
Amid the abjects deigns to-day to move
Whom no man cared for.   If the cruel city
Still claims its thousands, by the outcasts stand
Pure men and women in a gentle band,
Linked in a ministry of Love and Pity.
No more the insensate State
Binds down the worker, to exaggerate
The unequal gifts of Fate,
But comes instead, some care for common good,

Some glimmering sense of growing brotherhood.
No more half deafened by the unresting loom,
Soulless as is the brute, the pallid children pine;
Nor hapless slaves, half naked, 'mid the gloom
And grime and squalor of the sunless mine,
The young girl-workers coarsen, but all take
Some modest gleam of knowledge, which may breed
The faith that is above, yet under, every creed,
And of these humble lives, one day shall make
True citizens indeed.

   Nor shall thy peoples' voice
Keep silence of the salutary change
Which brought the gift of fullest freedom down
To humble lives, whether by field or town:
The potent gift, and strange,
Which wakes alone the wider civic sense,
Which, more than knowledge, sobers heart and mind,

A Song of Empire.

And rich and poor in closer ties can bind,
And knits a nation firm in harmony!
Let civil broils and fiercer dissidence
Come—we are one. What care have we?
In speech, in action, we are free.
No mob law need we fear, or senseless anarchy,
And for all these rejoice.

What law for us has done,
For all our greater England 'neath the sun,
Let us do now, building on high a State
Of half the World confederate!
Sure, 'twere the noblest victory of mind
Thy scattered realms to bind;
To guide the toiling, hopeless feet
To where is work for all, and life is sweet;
To teach our millions their great heritage,
To call together high world-councils sage,

Strong as the Priest's, in this our island-home;
Then, though the armèd world shall come,
What care, what fear, have we,
Who, being free, are one; and, being one, are free?

If all the wide Earth brings our millions food,
And if our navies whiten every sea,
If we have rest and wider brotherhood,
All these began with thee;
And shall, if Heaven so will, still more increase
With thy remaining years, till blessèd Peace,
Half frighted from us now by grave alarms
Of half a world in arms,
Shall brood, a white-winged Angel, o'er the Earth.
Then may the rule of Wrong be done!
Then may a new and Glorious Sun
Gild the illumined World! and then
Come Righteousness to men!

Three sovereigns of our English line
Have reached thy length of rule, each of his name the
    third,
But never England's heart was stirred
By those as 'tis by thine.
Our Henry died lonely and girt with foes;
Our greater Edward fell in dotage ere life's close;
And he thy grandsire knew a troublous time,
A dim pathetic figure! full of pain
And care too great for mortal to sustain,
And in his rayless sorrow grown sublime!

    Three Queens have swayed
Our England's fortunes—great Elizabeth,
In whose brave times the blast of war
Blew loud and fierce and far.
Her dauntless sailors dared the unbounded West,
And fought the Armada's might, and did prevail,

And wheresoe'er was seen an English sail
Her Empire was confest;
And round her gracious throne immortal flowers of song
Bloomed beautiful, bloomed long,
And left our English tongue as sweet as it was strong.

   And when a century and more had passed
In blood and turmoil, came a Queen at last.
Her soldiers and her sailors once again
Conquered on tented field and on the main,
And once more rose tho choir of song;
Not as the Elizabethan, deep and strong,
But, tripping lightly on its jewelled feet,
Issued politely sweet,
And Shakespeare's tongue and Milton's learned to dance
The minuet of France.

And now again once more
A Queen reigns o'er us as before ;
Again by land and sea
We cast the chequered sum of victory.
Once more our English tongue
Wakes to unnumbered bursts of song.
A great choir lifts again its accents fair,
And to those greater singers, if we find
To-day no answering mind,
'Tis that too large the Present fills the view,
Yet has its great names too.
Part of the glorious fellowship are we
The great Victorian company,
Which, since old Caëdmon's deep voice carolled strong,
Through England's chequered story bore along
The high pure fire of the world's sweetest song.

But not in the increase
Of Empire, or the victories of peace,
Chiefly we seek thy praise.
But that thy long and gracious days,
Lived in the solitude that hems a throne,
Since thy great sorrow came and left thee lone,
Were ever white, and free from thought of blame.
Not once in thy long years shadow of envy came
On thee, or him, whose stainless manhood bore
Thy love's unfading flower. Never before
In all our England was a royal home
Whereto the loving thoughts of humble hearts might come.
Thy children's children stand around thy knees,
Their children come in turn as fair as these ;
Thy people and thy children turn to thee,
Knit all in one by bonds of sympathy
With thee, our Queen, are we ;
Therefore we make our solemn jubilee !

A Song of Empire.

Flash, festal fires, high on the joyous air!
Clash, joy-bells! joy-guns, roar! and, jubilant trumpets,
    blare!
Let the great noise of our rejoicing rise!
Gleam, long-illumined cities, to the skies
Round all the earth, in every clime,
So far your distance half confuses time!
As in the old Judæan history,
Fling wide the doors and set the prisoners free!
Wherever England is o'er all the world,
Fly, banner of Royal England, stream unfurled!
The proudest Empire that has been, to-day
Rejoices and makes solemn jubilee.
For England! England! we our voices raise!
Our England! England! England! in our Queen we
    praise!
We love not war, but only peace,
Yet never shall our England's power decrease!

Whoever guides our helm of State,

Let all men know it, England shall be great!

We hold a vaster Empire than has been!

Nigh half the race of man is subject to our Queen!

Nigh half the wide, wide earth is ours in fee!

And where her rule comes, all are free.

And therefore 'tis, oh Queen, that we,

Knit fast in bonds of temperate liberty,

Rejoice to-day, and make our solemn jubilee!!

SELECTIONS FROM THE NOTICES

OF THE

POETICAL WORKS

OF

LEWIS MORRIS.

SONGS OF TWO WORLDS.

THESE poems were originally published in three volumes, issued in the years 1872, 1874, and 1875. The following are a few selections from the Press notices which appeared as they were issued.

FIRST SERIES.

"No one, after reading the first two poems—almost perfect in rhythm and all the graceful reserve of true lyrical strength—could doubt for an instant that this book is the result of lengthened thought and assiduous training in poetic forms. These poems will assuredly take high rank among the class to which they belong."—*British Quarterly Review*, April, 1872.

"If this volume is the mere prelude of a mind growing in power, we have in it the promise of a fine poet. . . . In 'The Wandering Soul,' the verse describing Socrates has that highest note of critical poetry, that in it epigram becomes vivid with life, and life reveals its inherent paradox. It would be difficult to describe the famous irony of Socrates in more poetical and more accurate words than by saying that he doubted men's doubts away."—*Spectator*, February 17th, 1872.

"In all this poetry there is a purity and delicacy of feeling which comes over one like morning air."—*Graphic*, March 16th, 1872.

OPINIONS OF THE PRESS.

SECOND SERIES.

"In earnestness, sweetness, and the gift of depicting nature, the writer may be pronounced a worthy disciple of his compatriot, Henry Vaughan, the Silurist. Several of the shorter poems are instinct with a noble purpose and a high ideal of life. One perfect picture, marginally annotated, so to speak, in the speculations which it calls forth, is 'The Organ-Boy.' But the most noteworthy poem is the 'Ode on a Fair Spring Morning,' which has somewhat of the charm and truth to nature of 'L'Allegro' and 'Il Penseroso.' It is the nearest approach to a master-piece in the volume."—*Saturday Review*, May 30th, 1874.

"This volume is a real advance on its predecessor of the same name, and contains at least one poem of great originality, as well as many of much tenderness, sweetness, and beauty. 'The Organ-Boy' we have read again and again, with fresh pleasure on every reading. It is as exquisite a little poem as we have read for many a day."—*Spectator*, June 13th, 1874.

"The reception of the New Writer's first series shows that, in his degree, he is one of the poetical forces of the time. Of the school of poetry of which Horace is the highest master, he is a not undistinguished pupil."—*Academy*, August 11th, 1874.

"The verses are full of melodious charm, and sing themselves almost without music."—*Blackwood's*, August 1st, 1874.

THIRD SERIES.

"Not unworthy of its predecessors. It presents the same command of metre and diction, the same contrasts of mood, the same grace and sweetness. It cannot be denied that he has won a definite position among contemporary poets."—*Times*, October 16th, 1875.

"'Evensong' shows power thought, and courage to grapple with the profoundest problems. In the 'Ode to Free Rome' we find worthy treatment of the subject and passionate expression of generous sympathy."—*Saturday Review*, July 31st, 1875.

"More perfect in execution than either of its predecessors. . . . The pure lyrics are sweeter and richer. In the 'Birth of Verse' every stanza is a little poem in itself, and yet a part of a perfect whole."—*Spectator*, May 22nd, 1875.

"If each book that he publishes is to mark as steady improvement as have his second and third, the world may surely look for something from the writer which shall immortalize him and remain as a treasure to literature."—*Graphic*, June 1st, 1875.

THE EPIC OF HADES.

BOOK II.*

"Fresh, picturesque, and by no means deficient in intensity; but the most conspicuous merits of the author are the judgment and moderation with which his poem is designed, his self-possession within his prescribed limits, and the unfailing elegance of his composition, which shrinks from obscurity, exuberance, and rash or painful effort as religiously as many recent poets seem to cultivate such interesting blemishes. . . . Perhaps the fine bursts of music in Marsyas, and the varied emotions portrayed in Andromeda, are less characteristic of the author than the prompt, yet graceful, manner in which he passes from one figure to another. . . . Fourteen of these pieces written in blank verse which bears comparison with the very best models make up a thoroughly enjoyable little volume. . . ."—*Pall Mall Gazette*, March 10th, 1876.

"It is natural that the favourable reception given to his 'Songs of Two Worlds' should have led the author to continue his

---

* Book II. was issued as a separate volume prior to the publication of Books I. and III. and of the complete work.

poetical exercises, and it is, no doubt, a true instinct which has led him to tread the classic paths of song. In his choice of subject he has not shrunk from venturing on ground occupied by at least two Victorian poets. In neither case need he shrink from comparison. His Marsyas is full of fine fancy and vivid description. His Andromeda has to us one recommendation denied to Kingsley's—a more congenial metre; another is its unstrained and natural narrative."—*Saturday Review*, May 20th, 1876.

"In his enterprise of connecting the Greek myth with the high and wider meaning which Christian sentiment naturally finds for it, his success has been great. The passage in which Apollo's victory over Marsyas and its effect are described is full of exquisite beauty. It is almost as fine as verse on such a subject could be. . . . The little volume is delightful reading. From the first line to the last, the high and delicate aroma of purity breathes through the various spiritual fables."—*Spectator*, May 27th, 1876.

"The blank verse is stately, yet sweet, free, graceful, and never undignified. We confidently believe that our readers will agree with us in regarding this as one of the finest and most suggestive poems recently published. We trust to have, ere long, more poetic work from his hand."—*British Quarterly Review*, April 1st, 1876.

"The writer has shown himself more critical than his friends, and the result is a gradual, steady progress in power, which we frankly acknowledge. . . . This long passage studded with graces."—*Academy*, April 29th, 1876.

BOOKS I. and III. and the COMPLETE WORK.

"In one sense the idea of his Epic is not only ambitious, but audacious, for it necessarily awakens reminiscences of Dante. Not unfrequently he is charmingly pathetic, as in his Helen and Psyche. There is considerable force and no small imagination in the description of some of the tortures in the 'Tartarus.' There is genuine poetical feeling in the 'Olympus.' . . . We might invite attention to many other passages. But it is more easy to give honest general praise than to single out particular extracts."—*Times*, February 9th, 1877.

"The whole of this last portion of the poem is exceedingly beautiful. . . . Nor will any, except critics of limited view, fail to recognize in the Epic a distinct addition to their store of those companions of whom we never grow tired."—*Athenæum*, March 3rd, 1877.

"We believe that the Epic will approve itself to students as one of the most considerable and original feats of recent English poetry."—*Saturday Review*, March 31st, 1877.

"Thought, fancy, music, and penetrating sympathy we have here, and that radiant, unnamable suggestive delicacy which enhances the attraction with each new reading."—*British Quarterly Review*, April, 1877.

"The present work is by far his greatest achievement; the whole tone of it is noble, and portions, more especially the concluding lines, are excessively beautiful."—*Westminster Review*, April, 1877.

"The work is one of which any singer might justly be proud. In fact, the Epic is in every way a remarkable poem, which to be appreciated must not only be read, but studied."—*Graphic*, March 10th, 1877.

"We do not hesitate to advance it as our opinion that 'The Epic of Hades' will enjoy the privilege of being classed amongst the poems in the English language which will live."—*Civil Service Gazette*, March 17th, 1877.

"Exquisite beauty of melodious verse. . . . A remarkable poem, both in conception and execution. We sincerely wish for the author a complete literary success."—*Literary World*, March 30th, 1877.

OPINIONS OF THE PRESS.

"Will live as a poem of permanent power and charm. It will receive high appreciation from all who can enter into its meaning, for its graphic and liquid pictures of external beauty, the depth and truth of its purgatorial ideas, and the ardour, tenderness, and exaltation of its spiritual life."—*Spectator*, May 5th, 1877.

"I have lately been reading a poem which has interested me very much, a poem called 'The Epic of Hades.' Many of you may never have heard of it; most of you may never have seen it. It is, as I view it, another gem added to the wealth of the poetry of our language."—*Mr. Bright's speech on Cobden, at Bradford*, July 25th, 1877.

"In the blank verse of the 'Epic of Hades,' apt words are so simply arranged with unbroken melody, that if the work were printed as prose, it would remain a song, and every word would still be where the sense required it; not one is set in a wrong place through stress of need for a mechanical help to the music. The poem has its sound mind housed in a sound body."—PROFESSOR MORLEY *in the Nineteenth Century*, February, 1878.

"I have read the 'Epic of Hades,' and find it truly charming. Its pictures will long remain with me, and the music of its words."—OLIVER WENDELL HOLMES, April, 1884.

THE EPIC OF HADES.

ILLUSTRATED QUARTO EDITION.

"Of Mr. Chapman's illustrations it is pleasant to be able to speak with considerable admiration, not only because they are a fortunate echo of the verse, and represent the feelings and incidents of the 'Epic,' but because of their intrinsic merits. There is in them a fine and high inspiration of an indefinite sort."—*Athenæum*, March 29th, 1879.

OPINIONS OF THE PRESS.

"'The Epic of Hades' is certainly one of the most remarkable works of the latter half of the nineteenth century. Here is an *édition de luxe* which may possibly tempt the unthinking to search for the jewel within the casket."—*World*, February 12th, 1879.

"The exquisite aërial feeling of 'Eros and Psyche,'—by far the best of the drawings,—in which the figures seem literally to float in ether. 'Laocoon' is grand and dignified, and all deserve to be noticed with attention."—*Graphic*, January 25th, 1879.

"These designs of themselves would be of the highest value, and when they are placed, as in this book, by way of illustration of a text which is full of power, their value is not easily estimated. The book ought to be one of the most cherished gifts that any lover of poetry or the pencil could desire."—*Scotsman*, January 23rd, 1879.

"The author has been most fortunate in his illustrator. The designs are gems of drawing and conception, and the mezzotint is admirably adapted to the style of drawing and subject. This is truly a charming addition to the literary table. It is seldom one sees figure illustrations of such graceful and powerful beauty, and so thoroughly in sympathy with the visionary subjects of the author."—*Art Journal*, April, 1879.

"'The Epic of Hades' has already won a place among the immortals. The lovely and terrible figures of the Greek mythology have never received a more exquisite consecration than at the hands of the author, who, with the true divination of the poet, has known how to interpret in the modern spirit the profound and pathetic fables of antiquity without vulgarizing by modern affectations their divine simplicity. This beautiful poem appears now in an *édition de luxe*—a setting not unworthy of such gems. The designs are noteworthy for their tenderness of sentiment and their languid grace."—*Daily News*, April 2nd, 1879.

GWEN:

A DRAMA IN MONOLOGUE.

"The charm of this beautiful little poem is its perfect simplicity of utterance; its chastened and exquisite grace. There is nothing very new in the incidents or in the characters of this most touching story, except in its unconventional ending, which takes the reader by surprise. The genius of the author has closed an idyll of love and death with a strain of sweet, sad music in that minor key which belongs to remembrance and regret."—*Daily News*, January 22nd, 1879.

"We have read this new work with the interest arising from the expectations which the author had quickened in us, and with the hope of finding those expectations confirmed. We are not disappointed, for we have here the same selectness of language, the same high, pure tone, the same delicate power of touching the deeper chords of thought and feeling, which have previously won our attention and sympathy."—*Literary World*, January 17th, 1879.

"At the close of the tale the heart swells with pathos, and the tears all but force their way into the eyes. To turn from the most noteworthy of modern poetry to the verse in which 'Gwen' is written is like turning from a brilliant painting to a fine statue. We are scarcely sensible of want of colour, so refreshed are we by purity of outline. All, indeed, is graceful, good, and poetical work, as pure and limpid in flow as a brook."—*Sunday Times*, February 2nd, 1879.

"The piece as a whole will repay very attentive perusal, while here and there in it there is a particular choice bit of work. Here, for example, is a fine lyric . . . and here a love-song of rare and exquisite beauty."—*New York Evening Post*, February 20th, 1879.

"Few among the later poets of our time have received such a generous welcome as the author. He has been appreciated not by critics alone, but by the general public. . . . The charm of 'Gwen' is to be found in the limpid clearness of the versification, in the pathetic notes which tell the old story of true love wounded and crushed. Nothing can be more artistically appropriate or more daintily melodious than the following. . . ."— *Pall Mall Gazette*, October 8th, 1879.

"The poem is, as a whole, tender, simple, chaste in feeling, and occasionally it rises to a lyrical loftiness of sentiment or grows compact with vigorous thought."—*New York "Nation,"* March 27th, 1879.

"The writer has gained inspiration from themes which inspired Dante; he has sung sweet songs and musical lyrics and whether writing in rhyme or blank verse, has proved himself a master of his instrument. He knows, like all true poets, how to transmute what may be called common into the pure gold of poetry."—*Spectator*, July 26th, 1879.

THE ODE OF LIFE.

"The 'Ode of Life' ought to be the most popular of all the author's works. People flock to hear great preachers, but in this book they will hear a voice more eloquent than theirs, dealing with the most important subjects that can ever occupy the thoughts of man."—*Westminster Review*, July, 1880.

"The many who have found what seemed to them of value and of use in the previous writings of the author, may confidently turn to this, his latest and, in his own view, his most mature work. It is full of beauty of thought, feeling, and language."— *Daily News*, April 8th, 1880.

"Full of exquisite taste, tender colour, and delicate fancy, these poems will add considerably to the reputation of their author."—*Sunday Times*, April 25th, 1880.

"The author is one of the few real poets now living. Anything at once more sympathetic and powerful it would be difficult to find in the poetry of the present day."—*Scotsman*, May 11th, 1880.

"Next to the 'Epic of Hades,' it is his best work."—*Cambridge Review*, May 19th, 1880.

"Here is one standing high in power and in fame who has chosen a nobler course. . . . The experiment is successful, and though we must not now discuss the laws to which the structure of an ode should conform, we rank the poem in this respect as standing far above Dryden's celebrated composition, but below the Odes of Wordsworth on Immortality and of Milton on the Nativity, which still remain peerless and without a rival."—*Congregationalist*, May 1st, 1880.

"A high devout purpose and wide human sympathy ennoble all the writer's work, and his clear language and quiet music will retain his audience."—*Nineteenth Century*, August, 1880.

"In all that respects technical points, certainly the most finished work we have yet had from the author's hand, and here and there the phrasing is exquisite. For ambitious aims, and for art which so far has justified those aims, for elevation and refinement, these poems are in advance of any of the author's former works."—*British Quarterly Review*, July, 1880.

"Any notice of recent poetry would be inadequate without a reference to the 'Ode of Life.' The only fault we have to find with this really remarkable effort—a sort of expansion of Wordsworth's famous Ode—is that it is rather too long for its ideas; but it possesses power, sweetness, occasional profundity, and unmistakable music. It is, when all is said and done, a true 'Ode,' sweeping the reader along as the ode should do, and

'Growing like Atlas, stronger for its load.'

It appears to us to bring definite proof that the writer's pretensions have not been over-stated."—*Contemporary Review*, February, 1881.

SONGS UNSUNG.

"Some of the more important pieces make almost equal and very high demands alike on my sympathy and my admiration, and I hope you may long be enabled to cherish the enviable gift of finding utterance for Truths so deep in forms of so much power and beauty."—*Letter from* Mr. GLADSTONE, November, 1883.

"The reader of his former work will probably commence this volume with considerable expectations. Nor will he be altogether disappointed, although he will probably wish that Mr. Morris had given the world more of his exquisite classical workmanship."—*Fortnightly Review*, November, 1883.

"'The New Creed' is, in some respects, his most striking achievement. The poem is one well suited to his mind, but we are not aware that he has ever before written anything at once so impressive, so solemn, and so self-restrained. The last two lines have all the happy energy of the highest poetry."—*Spectator*, November 10th, 1883.

"In reading it one feels constantly 'How worthy this book would be of beautiful illustrations!'"—*Academy*, November 24th, 1883.

"The volume is full of the sweet fruits of a large experience; a profound study of the many problems of life; a clear insight into human nature; and the book as a whole ranks among the best gifts which the press has in recent years bestowed upon us."—*Leeds Mercury*, November 21st, 1883.

"There is not one of these 'Songs Unsung' which does not deserve to be read and re-read."—*Glasgow Herald*, November 16th, 1883.

"In Mr. Morris's new volume we recognize the old qualities which are so dear to his wide circle of admirers."—*Daily News*, December 4th, 1883.

"We may safely predict as warm a welcome for the new volume as has been accorded to its predecessors."—*Ecclesiastical Gazette*, November 15th, 1883.

"Those who have followed Mr. Morris's career will be pleased to find that his poetic grasp, his argumentative subtlety, his tenderness of sympathetic observation, his manly earnestness, are as conspicuous and impressive as before."—Mr. BAYNE, *in the Helensburgh Times.*

"The reputation earned by the author's books has been such as few men in a century are permitted to enjoy. Beginning with the first volume, it has gone on increasing."—*Liverpool Mercury*, November 9th, 1883.

"For ourselves we dare hardly say how high we rank Mr. Morris. This last volume is deserving of highest praise. In some of its contents no living poet, to our mind, can surpass him."—*Oxford University Herald*, March 8th, 1884.

"The gems of this volume, to our mind, are some of the shorter poems, which are full of melody and colour, saturated with lyrical feeling, and marked by that simplicity without which no poem of this class can be called great."—*British Quarterly Review*, January, 1884.

OPINIONS OF THE PRESS.

"The writer is never diffuse or vague or pointless, both his road and the end of it are always in view."—*New York Critic*, January 19th, 1884.

"In one sense 'Songs Unsung' is more typical of Mr. Morris's genius than any of his previous works. There is in them the same purity of expression, the same delicate fancy, the same mastery of technique, and withal the same loftiness of conception."—*Scotsman*, December 22nd, 1883.

"In some respects we must award him the distinction of having a clearer perception of the springs of nineteenth-century existence than any of his contemporaries. . . . What could be more magnificent than the following conception of the beginning of things. . . ."—*Whitehall Review*, October, 1883.

"Mr. Morris has always that picturesque power which limns in a few words a suggestive and alluring picture of nature or of life evoking the imagination of the reader to supplement the clear and vigorous work of the poet."—*New York Christian Union*, February, 1884.

"No lover of poetry will fail to make himself possessed of this volume from the pen of one who has made for himself so high and distinctive a place among modern writers."—*Manchester Examiner*, January 31st, 1884.

"After making every possible deduction, 'Songs Unsung' is a noble volume, and ought to be received by those who, like ourselves, believe in the necessary subordination of art to morality with profound gratification."—*Freeman*, April 18th, 1884.

"We have quoted enough to show that this book has genuine merit in it, merit in poetry, merit in philosophy, and, we may add, merit in religion. Lewis Morris takes the 'new and deeper view of the world' of which Carlyle now and then caught sunny glimpses. He sings in sweet and measured Tennysonian strains of philosophy what Darwin and Herbert Spencer teach in prose;

without the informing glow of the imagination. There are living poets greater than Lewis Morris, but of the younger race of poets he is foremost."—*The Inquirer*, April 5th, 1884.

" The hold which a poet who writes with such intense seriousness of purpose and such passionate earnestness gains upon his generation is far stronger and more lasting than if his sole attempt were to stimulate or to satisfy the sense of the beautiful. All the things of which we wish that poetry should speak to us, have voice given to them in the song of this glorious singer."—*South Australian Advertiser*, March 24th, 1884.

"As a whole this volume, while charming anew the poet's former admirers, should win for his genius a wider acquaintance and appreciation."—*Boston Literary World*, February 23rd, 1884.

" Mr. Morris has the invaluable gift of recognizing and being in full sympathy with the current ideas and feelings of the time. The broad humanitarianism, the genuine sympathy with the sufferings of the poor and unfortunate, characteristic of our age, is one of the most attractive features of his poetry, and to the revival of the feeling for classical beauty, which may be looked upon as a collateral branch of the 'æsthetic' movement, he owes more than one charming inspiration. . . . To sum up. Mr. Morris's volume is likely to add to his reputation. It is healthy in tone, and shows no decline of the varied qualities to which the author owes his widespread reputation."—*Times*, June 9, 1884.

GYCIA.

"'Gycia' abounds in powerful dramatic situations, while the intricate evolutions of a double plot in love and statecraft provoke perpetual curiosity, which is only fully satisfied at the end. The heroine, in her single-minded patriotism and her undeviating devotion to duty, rises to the level of the loftiest feminine conceptions of the old Greek dramatists. And she is finely contrasted with her generous and impulsive husband, who has neither her sternness of principle nor her steadiness of purpose. The form of the verse is so picturesque, and the flow is so free, that we should say, if effectively delivered, it must command an appreciative audience. It would have been difficult for any poet to do full justice to the thrilling scene where Gycia denounces the treason of her husband and his countrymen to the chief magistrates of the State. Yet Mr. Morris has done it well. Nearly as stirring, and even more pathetic, is the scene where the pair are seated side by side in state, with anguished hearts and smiling faces, at the banquet, which, as each knows well, is to end with a horrible catastrophe."—*Times*, October 18th, 1886.

"The *dramatis personæ* have life and individuality; the situations are for the most part strong and rich in really dramatic effects; the architecture of the plot is simple, harmonious, and symmetrical, without any of that obtrusive artificiality which often accompanies symmetry;

and the action never drags, but is always in determinate progressive movement. A drama of which these things can be truthfully said is not merely good as drama, but has that element of popularity which is of more practical value than the absolute goodness of which only critics take account. The verse is, throughout, strong, fluent, rich, variously expressive, and adequate with that adequacy which satisfies without drawing attention to itself."—MR. J. A. NOBLE, *in the Academy*, November 20th, 1886.

"Throughout there is the artistic contrast and striving between the spirit of liberty and of tyranny, between Republican simplicity and patrician form and ceremony, and a great political lesson is taught. It is hardly necessary to praise the nobility and the dignity, the sweetness and the strength, of Mr. Morris's verse. 'Gycia' will add to his already firmly founded reputation as a dramatic poet and writer of noble blank verse. It is one of the few works by recent English poets that seems capable of thrilling an audience upon the stage, as well as enchaining the mind of the student in the chamber."—*Scotsman*, November 10th, 1886.

"I have lost no time in reading your tragedy. I perused it with great interest, and a sense throughout of its high poetic power."—*Letter from* MR. GLADSTONE, October 20th, 1886.

www.ingramcontent.com/pod-product-compliance
Lightning Source LLC
Chambersburg PA
CBHW020910230426
43666CB00008B/1399